MEDIATED TRANSCENDENCE

MED

TRANSCE

A Postmode

Mercer
University Press

ATED

NDENCE

rn Reflection

Jerry Gill

ISBN 0-86554-318-6 [casebound edition]
ISBN 0-86554-348-8 [paperback edition]

∞

The paper used in this publication meets
the minimum requirements of American National Standard
for Information Sciences—Permanence of Paper
for Printed Library Materials, ANSI Z39.48-1984.

Library of Congress Cataloging-in-Publication Data
Gill, Jerry H.
Mediated transcendence.

1. Transcendence (Philosophy)   I. Title.
BD362.G55   1989   141'.3   88-29667
ISBN 0-86554-318-6 [casebound] ISBN 0-86554-348-8 [paperback]

CONTENTS

for

MARI

my Indian Summer . . .

PREFACE

A preface gives an author an opportunity to acknowledge the various persons who have contributed to publication of his or her book. This is an appropriate and happy task, at least for me, since thinking and writing are never done in isolation, but develop in dialogue. I am pleased to express my gratitude to those "significant others" who helped make this book a reality.

My colleagues Bert Fay and Bruce Johnston not only have provided me with a professional home at the College of Saint Rose, but see to it, by means of friendship and discussion, that I continue to grow here. My wife and colleague, Mari Sorri, has enabled me to shape my ideas more clearly and thoroughly. Finally, Susan Carini, at Mercer University Press, has shown a great deal of understanding and persistence in transforming my original manuscript into the present volume.

By no stretch of the imagination do I consider this study the definitive treatment of the subject of transcendence. Thirty-five years of wrestling with this and related issues do, I hope, ensure that my treatment of the topic is knowledgeable, clear, and constructive—and perhaps even provocative.

One

INTRODUCTION

The Loss

of Transcendence

1. Traditional Dualism or Modern Naturalism?

It is clear that we stand today at a crossroads with respect to the notion of transcendence. On every hand there are those who accept the loss of transcendence, whether reluctantly or gratefully, advocating the development of science, philosophy, and even theology within the structures and strictures of a naturalist framework, one that functions strictly according to the "horizontal" dimension of human existence. In opposition to such "humanism," there remain a few ardent supporters of a return to the traditional dualistic worldview, according to which the horizontal realm of reality is explained in terms of the "vertical" or transcendent realm. Such thinkers generally speak in terms of returning to traditional "supernaturalism," both in relation to science and theology, as well as to "absolute values" in the realms of morality, politics, and the arts.

The naturalist approach has a great deal to be said for it, especially when one considers the weaknesses of traditional dualism, both inherently and in practice. Generally the dualist approach has led to various forms of otherworldliness in which the two realms have at best been separated and defined as essentially different from each other. When this is done it becomes very difficult to negotiate a way for the transcendent to interact with the human realm in a meaningful fashion; for any such interaction will either be subject to certain human conditions and criteria by means of which it can be grasped and appropriated or it will not. In the former case, the sense in which such interaction can be said to involve the transcendent is obscured, since the conditions and criteria employed remain human and naturalistic. In the latter case, it becomes unclear how the transcendent could be recognized and acknowledged if the appropriate conditions and criteria are also transcendent and thus beyond human use and evaluation.

Naturalism, or "secular humanism" as it is sometimes designated, takes a wide variety of forms, from scientific reductionism and behaviorism, through social biology and dialectical materialism, to atheistic existentialism and logical empiricism. Even in the arts one can discern naturalistic tendencies in some advocates of such movements as expressionism, absurdism, and minimalism. Both structuralists and cognitive scientists on the one hand, as well as deconstructionists and phenomenologists on the other hand, generally assume that the exploration and examination of human existence and thought can and must proceed without any reference to the notion of transcendence.

Those who advocate a return to some form of traditional dualism as the only way to insure a proper place for transcendence are neither so numerous nor so diverse, but their position is always lurking in the background nonetheless. Creationists and followers of Jerry Falwell on the one hand, fideists and Reformed theologians on the other hand, all urge an unapologetic return to traditional supernaturalist categories and values. They are joined by neo-Thomist theologians and neoconservative political thinkers, as well as by "back-to-basics" educators and some radical peace activists. In each of these movements—in diverse ways to be sure— the transcendent is conceived of as standing *above* or *behind* human and natural reality, both supporting and intervening in it. This view is worth noting, if only because its rival has a definite tendency to leave us with a one-dimensional, relativist account of human existence.

Where does all this leave us? Are we forced to choose between these two alternatives or is there another angle of approach? It is the purpose of this present study to suggest that there is, indeed, another and more helpful approach to the question of transcendence. It does not matter whether we construe this alternative approach as a third option that slips between the horns of the dilemma as outlined above, as a form of taking the bull by the horns and denying the assumptions upon which the dilemma is based. What does matter is that we come to understand that the debate between traditional dualism and contemporary naturalism is misconceived and thus unnecessary. Moreover, my own proposal is that transcendence can be construed in such a manner as to be compatible with the positive insights and concerns of both of the current angles of approach, while avoiding the difficulties and liabilities of each.

The axis of my proposal is the notion of *mediation,* not in the sense of compromise but in the sense of the dynamic whereby intangible reality can be said to be encountered and conveyed *in and through* the particulars constituting tangible reality. The intangible reality mediated by means of tangible reality neither exists nor is known independently of the particulars of the tangible, but at the same time it cannot be reduced to an account of those particulars. If transcendence is thought of as intangible reality mediated in and through the horizontal dimension of human and natural existence, it can serve as a meaningful concept in both philosophy and religion. In short, the seeming loss of transcendence can be overcome by rethinking at the outset what is meant by the notion.

The supporting considerations whose orbits locate the axis of my proposal are in no way esoteric or novel. Rather, they are drawn from the general structure of everyday experience, whether in perception, interpersonal and social relations, aesthetics, or morality. In all such areas of human endeavor, what is real, true, and valuable is mediated to us in and through our natural experience. The increasingly rich and comprehensive aspects of the world are discerned and encountered by means of our interaction with them in the push-and-pull of everyday life. The same holds true for our awareness of the transcendent. Rather than discarding the notion of transcendence as obsolete or affirming a return to traditional dualism, I am proposing that the notion be recovered by reconceiving of the relationship between it and the natural.

There are four orbits or phases constituting the following proposal. The first (chapter two) pertains to "what there is," to general ontological and metaphysical questions. The task here is to overcome the gap between traditional dualism and contemporary naturalism by construing reality as composed of a number of simultaneously interpenetrating dimensions, rather than mutually exclusive realms. These dimensions are seen as structured hierarchically according to their degree of richness and comprehensiveness, with each being mediated by and mediating those beneath and above it, respectively.

The second orbit (chapter three) concerns how these mediated dimensions of reality can be known. The stress is on the centrality of interaction to all knowledge and on the fundamental priority of tacit knowing over explicit knowing. Attention is also given to the social character of knowledge and the importance of the distinction between verification and confirmation.

The third orbit (chapter four) relates to the question of moral value or "What should I do?" Here again, the concern is to show how values can be understood as mediated in and through the particulars constituting the relational and contextual situation, while nonetheless transcending them. Emphasis is placed on achieving a balance between relevance and tradition by means of dialogue and persuasion. In this way ethical values can be viewed as transcendent without becoming static and doctrinaire.

The final orbit (chapter five) centers on the distinction between "what can be said" and what must "show itself," on the nature and function of language. The focus here is on speech as a social activity rather than a propositional mirroring of states of affairs. By means of speech-acts we interact with, alter, and create our worlds of meaning. Moreover, at the deepest level language is essentially a metaphoric activity. Thus, meaning is mediated through function and the metaphoric mode. Transcendent meaning, then, can be seen as communicated in and through the uses to which we put our everyday speech, especially at the fundamental, metaphoric level.

In the concluding chapter I treat the significance of the notion of *transcendence as mediated* for the idea of God's activity in the world. This entire proposal is meant as an invitation to alter one's perspective with respect to the notion of transcendence. Its tone is hence one of dialogue and persuasion, not one of knock-down, drag-out demonstration. It is this invitational mode that constitutes the postmodern character of these reflections. I am proposing that the time has come to "put away childish ways" of speaking. To continue with Paul's line of thought, although someday we may encounter and know the transcendent "face to face," we currently experience it as mediated through the glass of everyday, natural reality. That such mediation is both possible and sufficient, though limited, is the burden of the reflections that follow.

That which is to be rethought must first, obviously, have become problematic. So it is appropriate that we begin with a consideration of the loss of transcendence as a viable concept in modern and contemporary thought. The loss in question did not occur overnight or willy-nilly, but slowly and dialectically as a result of a long ideational struggle among the dominant thinkers in Western philosophy and theology. My tracing the main developments within the history of this struggle will set the stage for my proposal regarding the possible recovery of transcendence. This tracing will also provide us with the best working definition of what is meant by the notion of transcendence, since efforts to define one's key terms at the outset generally only succeed in begging the crucial issues at stake.

2. Plato, Aristotle, and Medieval Thought

Although it is debatable whether or not Plato was a Platonist, it is clear that there are passages in his dialogues that seem to lend support to the traditional interpretation of his thought, especially as it pertains to the "theory of Forms." The objects of actual knowledge, according to Plato, can only be the pure, eternal, abstract concepts that lie behind or beyond the particular objects and events constituting our everyday world of perceptual experience. A specific horse is only a horse by virtue of the fact and to the degree to which it participates in or resembles the essence or formal defining qualities of "horseness." Thus, not only is our knowledge of this particular horse dependent on a (preexistent?) knowledge of the Form of Horseness, but the very being of specific horses is likewise dependent on the prior existence of this abstract Form.

Of course, both in Plato's works and in Western thought, to say nothing of everyday life, interest is generally focused on more important concepts than that of horseness. The concern is with such realities as Beauty, Virtue, Knowledge, and Justice. The point, however, is the same, namely that the being and knowledge of such Forms is in some sense *transcendent to* or *independent of* the particulars of the world of ordinary, especially perceptual experience. For Plato, or at least for Platonism, these Forms were thought of as abstract, unchanging concepts or definitions that would seem to exist independently of both the material world and individual minds, though they can be known by the latter by means of arduous and careful analysis.

According to this view, the world is divided into two main realms, Being and becoming. The former, the truly Real, is the realm of unchanging, formal definition and purely abstract reason, while the latter is the realm of transient reflections and unreliable sensory beliefs. Thus we have a two-story world in which the top floor, the domain of all that is Real, True, and Good, transcends and in no way depends upon the bottom floor. In fact, the only interaction between these two realms is unilateral and passive in nature; the lower world *reflects* the higher world, but the latter is oblivious to and independent of the lower world.

It is interesting that Aristotle, Plato's most brilliant student, came to disagree with his teacher over precisely this issue of whether these two aspects of the world can, in fact, exist as separate domains. While he agreed with Plato that for the purposes of defining and attaining ultimate reality and knowledge Formal reality was necessary, Aristotle also maintained that this reality can neither exist nor be known independently of the objects and activities constituting perceptual reality and experience. For Aristotle, the source of what is real and knowable is not transcendent of the everyday world of things and observations. On the contrary, he argued that it is only by means of examination of and inductive generalization from such phenomena that we can come to any knowledge whatsoever of the higher, Formal, or conceptual reality. Moreover, for Aristotle, the Form of Horseness or Beauty actually and only exists *in* particular horses and beautiful objects; for him, the two are inseparable and interdependent.

Things got a bit more complicated, to be sure, when Aristotle went on to develop his metaphysical theories more specifically. In particular, he ended up arguing that God is the "final cause" or raison d'être of the world, the ultimate "unmoved mover" of all that is. Aristotle's God seems to have been more independent of and transcendent to the material world than Aristotle's basic posture would lead one to expect, since he defined God as "pure thought" whose only activity is "thinking about thinking," without in any way being involved actively in the world.

These fine points aside, a fundamental difference existed between the metaphysical theories of Plato and Aristotle with respect to the relationship between the material and conceptual aspects of the world and experience. Plato affirmed their essential diversity, as well as the superiority and independence of abstract, conceptual reality over the material, while Aristotle insisted on their interrelatedness and mutual dependency. Thus the stage was set for the controversy over the possibility and nature of transcendence that has served as one of the major foci of Western philosophy and theology right up to the present.

With the advent of the Christian religion, together with its incorporation of Greek and Roman modes of thought into its theological infrastructure, the question of the viability of the notion of transcendence became especially pressing. Initially the Platonic posture became dominant, perhaps because the general idea of a two- or even three-storied universe had already infiltrated Jewish thought (by way of Babylonian and Persian influences) at the time of the inception and formation of Christian community and Scriptures. This dominance of Platonic thought over Aristotelian was so complete that the latter was nearly lost altogether until the Muslim philosophers reintroduced it and Thomas Aquinas adopted and adapted it as the philosophical basis for his and nearly all subsequent Catholic theology.

Augustine was the medieval thinker who found in Plato's writings a philosophical expression of the theological truths of the Christian Scriptures. It seemed obvious to him that Plato's realm of Being, the residence of Formal, unchanging reality, was simply another way of talking about God's heavenly domain. Equally obvious was the inherent evil and deceptiveness of the material world, especially sensory experience. Thus Augustine affirmed Plato's basic dualism between mind and body, the latter being characterized as "the prisonhouse of the soul." True reality and value, as well as the knowledge thereof, transcend this world and perception. They can only be attained, according to Augustine, by means of inner, spiritual insight and discipline.

Some eight hundred years later, Thomas Aquinas sought to construct a Christian theology on the less dualistic, more "immanentalist" philosophy of Aristotle. To be sure, Aquinas had to modify certain of Aristotle's doctrines, such as the eternality of the universe and the disinterested character of God. The end result was a system of thought in which the controlling realities and values, while remaining qualitatively transcendent, were nonetheless far more inherent and integral to the material world, with its natural processes and perceptions, than was the case with Augustine. Nevertheless, Aquinas's overall approach remained dualistic in nature to the degree that God was viewed as transcendent of the world as its creator (efficient cause) and its director (formal cause). There thus were two main realms, the natural and the supernatural, the one being controlled by and incorporated into the other.

Perhaps the fundamental shift that distinguishes the modern era from the classical and medieval periods is that the "horizontal" dimension of existence is substituted for the "vertical" as the ground of value and reality. Since roughly the 1500s the natural and/or social aspects of the world increasingly have become the axis of human awareness and activity, while traditionally transcendent considerations have played an ever-diminishing role. The struggle between these two worldviews dominated the seventeenth, eighteenth, and nineteenth centuries. A brief review of this struggle will provide a helpful documentation of the process by means of which the notion of transcendence was lost.

3. Rationalism, Empiricism, and Kant

Modern rationalism—as distinguished from both the classical rationalism of Plato and the medieval affirmation of the transcendent—sought to locate the latter, not in the world of pure Being, but rather in the unchanging and unerring principles and procedures of rational inquiry. In establishing the right and necessity of each individual to know the truth for him/herself, the Continental rationalists at the same time located the notion of transcendence in the a priori truths that carry us beyond the merely empirical. Such truths provide us with knowledge of the ultimate structure of reality, thereby reiterating the metaphysical transcendence of classical and medieval thought, albeit from an epistemological point of departure.

One of the chief difficulties with this angle of approach is that it turned out to be capable of producing metaphysical systems that, while based on the same rationalistic principles, nonetheless remained mutually exclusive of one another. Starting from the supposedly self-evident truth, "I think, therefore I am," and proceeding according to such principles as the law of noncontradiction and the law of sufficient reason, Descartes constructed a dualistic account of the nature of reality and a theistic view of the divine. In the final analysis, Descartes's metaphysical system turned out to be quite "orthodox," leaving the concept of transcendence pretty much intact.

Spinoza, on the other hand, began with roughly the same rationalistic principles, coupled with a different definition of "substance," and ended up with a metaphysical system entirely different from Descartes's. Spinoza was a pantheistic monist rather than a dualist, and his concept of God was anything but orthodox. Moreover, the relation of Spinoza's pantheism to the concept of transcendence is awkward at best. While he stressed the inappropriateness of expecting God "to love you in return," thus pressing transcendence to what would seem to be its deistic limit, he also affirmed that God is immanent in all aspects and modes of reality.

Leibniz, in his turn, also began with principles similar to those of Descartes and Spinoza, yet he developed a metaphysical system that can only be termed "infinite pluralism." His universe of self-contained, perfectly coordinated monads acting independently of yet in absolute harmony with one another not only contrasts with the dualism of Descartes and the monism of Spinoza, but it renders the relationship between God and the rest of creation quite problematic. It seems difficult at best to know whether transcendence has survived in any recognizable form.

As is well known, the British empiricists were not much impressed with the forgoing rationalist maneuvers and sought to define and ground knowledge in sensory experience rather than in abstract rational principles. In spite of the fact that such a move would seem to rule out any notion of transcendence at the outset, nearly all of the empiricists sought to retain some place for it in their philosophy. Locke held out for the knowledge of God as demonstrable by reason, since it is clear that God cannot be experienced by the senses. He was as inconsistent with respect to this notion as he was with respect to the concept of substance, since the latter is also unexplainable according to strict empiricist principles. Moreover, Locke's deism extended the notion of transcendence well beyond orthodox theological limits.

Berkeley, of course, had his own way of construing empiricism so as to make room for, indeed to make indispensable, the transcendent. He argued that Locke was as ill advised to seek to ground knowledge in a world external to the human mind as he was to seek to *demonstrate* the existence of God. For Berkeley, it made more sense to posit God as the necessary and sufficient source of our sensations and resultant ideas: God was thus of the world. Unfortunately he never satisfactorily established the necessity of such a source nor disentangled God from the erroneous and evil ideas we frequently have. As a result transcendence got lost in the shuffle.

Hume was a more consistent empiricist than either Locke or Berkeley. Beginning with our sensations is all well and good, he argued, but went on to ask, How can we rationally justify going beyond them? Hume concluded, after much painstaking argumentation, that we have no rational basis for concluding that anything or anyone other than our own minds is the source of our sensations and ideas. Even the pattern of our experiences, especially that of causal relationships, cannot be established as necessary in and of itself. Not only can we not speak responsibly of *experiencing* God, we cannot legitimately infer God's existence from our experience either.

Moreover, Hume sought to show that all inductive arguments that seek to establish the existence of a transcendent being or reality are doomed to failure from the outset, since they all must admit conflicting evidence and the viability of other possible explanations. In fact, the very notion of transcendence is itself problematic, since by definition the transcendent is *beyond* human experience and therefore unknowable. In addition, Hume had already eliminated the possibility of establishing the existence of God deductively—by using the classical "proofs"—by means of his distinction between "relations of ideas" and "matters of fact." The latter, as just mentioned, can yield only probabilities about matters of experience, while the former can provide only judgments as to consistency among original ideas and definitions. Questions of existence lie completely outside the domain of deductive arguments.

Although he seems to have found the results of his own reasoning difficult to swallow, Hume is generally interpreted as standing by his skeptical conclusions, both with respect to knowledge of such things as objects external to the mind, the self, and other persons, and to the knowledge of God as well. However, he sought to retain the notion of transcendence by affirming that although belief in God cannot be justified rationally, it can be seen, and more properly so, as a commitment of *faith*. In fact, Hume sees skepticism as clearing the way for the viability of faith. With Kant, Hume could say, "I have set aside reason in order to make room for faith."

This discussion brings us to Kant himself. Having been awakened from his rationalistic slumbers by Hume, Kant set out (in his *Critique of Pure Reason*) to provide a rational basis for knowledge in both the formal and natural sciences. He grounded such knowledge in the structure of the human mind itself, in what he called "the categories of the understanding," rather than outside it in external objects or in God. For Kant, the mind is the medium or framework through which we construe reality; hence our experience and resultant knowledge are a function of the interaction between our minds and the world. Thus we can be said to have knowledge of reality as experienced by us, of what Kant called the "phenomena," since this is what it means to have a human mind at all. Our judgments concerning causal relationships, for instance, are legitimate, not because we can say that this is the way things are in reality, but because this is the way the human mind actually structures our experience.

Kant was prepared—indeed eager—to agree with Hume, however, that any knowledge of how the world is in and of itself, apart from the activity of our minds (what Kant called the "noumena"), is entirely out of the question. The reason for this conclusion is simple. Since knowledge, according to Kant's schema, is a function of the interaction of our minds and the world, any knowledge we have must necessarily be about the phenomenally real. To speak of knowing that which is by definition beyond the very conditions that render knowledge possible is to cut oneself off at the pockets. Thus for Kant, as well as for Hume, the concept of a transcendent God lies entirely outside the conditions of rationality and is therefore not a concept at all. In Kant's view, all proofs of God's existence founder on this crucial objection: rationality cannot reach beyond itself without contradicting itself.

Of course, the story does not end there, since Kant, too, went on to devise a way of speaking of the transcendent. Although the notion cannot be found a home within the bounds of "pure reason," it can—indeed must—be incorporated into our thinking about "practical reason." In his *Critique of Practical Reason*, Kant argued that our ethical activity and moral reasoning make no sense apart from certain "posits" that, while not rationally justifiable in the strict sense, are clearly reasonable in relation to moral behavior. Kant claimed that the reality of a transcendent lawgiver and judge, as well as the freedom necessary to responsibility, are presupposed by our sense of duty; to render moral judgments is to assume an absolute standard and a transcendent standard-setter. Thus "pure" rationality is set aside in order to make room for transcendence in the realm of "practical rationality."

4. Science, Hegel, and Existentialism

Kant's philosophy, as laid out in his first *Critique*, paralleled the developments that had taken place in the rise of the scientific method during the sixteenth, seventeenth, and eighteenth centuries. This is true in the following ways. First, scientific activity had gradually replaced the procedure of settling experiential questions by reference to authoritative sources, such as the Bible or Aristotle. This meant that those who sought knowledge were encouraged, nay required, to come to their own conclusions on the basis of their own or others' investigations. Knowledge and truth were made matters of public rather than private policy and interpretation; they became the property and concern of everyone, part and parcel of what it means to think.

Second, scientific activity, unlike authoritarianism, has built into it a systematic self-corrective process that sooner or later will ferret out those ideas and claims that are misleading and erroneous. Even if a would-be scientist tampers with the evidence or perpetrates a hoax, this will be discovered by other scientists (who are not "authorities" because all findings are open to, indeed invite, replication and analysis). This parallels Kant's use of reason to critique reason; both science and reason seek to establish knowledge as independent of traditions and pronouncements, as limited but adequate.

The third parallel pertains to the self-contained universe that results both from Kant's critique of pure reason and from scientific activity. In order to render our understanding of the world both meaningful and confirmable, it seems necessary to assume a "closed system" in which there are no inherently unpredictable or spontaneous events; otherwise our explanations will always be subject to capricious and ad hoc modification, thus becoming no explanations at all. The price to be paid for such consistency, however, is the impossibility of speaking about any sort of transcendent reality. The vertical dimension of traditional philosophies and theologies has been barred from the premises as a matter of necessary principle. This is akin to Kant's wall between the phenomenal and the noumenal.

In general, the increasing ascendency of scientific methodology served to push the notion of transcendence further from the center of the cognitive arena, finally removing it altogether. The notion could still be employed, however—perhaps even more appropriately so—in the realm of faith and practice, should one wish to do so. Thus the ever-growing dichotomy between science and religion, between fact and value, that has come to characterize our modern, especially our contemporary, cultural life. The only room left for such things as transcendence is in the realm of the personal, the "subjective," and the practical. Some bemoan this dichotomy in the name of integration, while others hail it as the true watershed of modern faith.

Not everyone, to be sure, was caught up in this effort to relocate the transcendent. Hegel's response to Kant, for example, was one of "business as usual." Following Fichte's lead, Hegel collapsed Kant's dichotomy between the phenomenal and noumenal worlds on the grounds that if Kant is correct, not only is the distinction itself unnecessary but it is impossible, since the world as we know it through our minds is all there really is. Thus Hegel concluded, "What is thought is real and what is real is thought." This position, far from resulting in yet another version of Berkeley's "subjective idealism," was transformed by Hegel into what has been termed "Absolute Idealism"—a philosophy that not only makes room for transcendence but one that majors in it.

For Hegel and his followers, both in the nineteenth and twentieth century, reality is a complex spiritual whole that "concretizes" itself in the historical and material world by means of a dialectical process that will lead eventually to the ultimate fulfillment of the Absolute Spirit. Such a conceptual framework is easily merged with the traditional theological categories of God's transcendent, creative involvement in the world. Many, including Hegel himself, have engaged in just such accommodation procedures in order to ground the notion of transcendence rationally and idealistically. In a way, this approach can be said to characterize much of modern liberal theology from Schleiermacher and Ritschl to Tillich and Teilhard de Chardin.

There are, however, at least two serious prices to be paid for seeking to establish the notion of transcendence in this way. The first is that such an approach tends to render spiritual reality "so heavenly minded as to be of no earthly good." Everything and everyone seem to get swallowed up in a vastly abstract and rationalistic system that has precious little "cash value" at the concrete level of human experience. We shall hear more of this criticism from the existentialist corner in a moment.

The second price to pay is even more inflationary. By the very act of ultimately raising everything to the spiritual, transcendent level of reality, one in fact does just the opposite. For, if each and every aspect of reality is but a part of the Absolute whole, then the very notion of transcendence would seem to be lost altogether. To put it differently, there is an inherent pantheism in the Hegelian approach to transcendence that is self-defeating. "Absolute Spirit" is, in the final analysis, far too immanent to allow for any viable concept of transcendence at all. Thus, in the end, there is not that much difference between Hegel, Kant, Hume, and modern science. Each in his own way renders transcendence inaccessible, whether deliberately or in an effort to salvage it.

It is into this quandary that the existentialists stepped, deliberately and with a vengeance. Both Nietzsche and Kierkegaard reacted negatively to Hegel's rationalistic, systematizing idealism, though each in a different direction. Both essentially sought to go back to Kant's moratorium on all human attempts to speak of and know the transcendent, although they affirmed quite opposite responses to it. Nietzsche urged us to turn our backs on the notion of the noumenal world in order to pay better attention, not to Kant's phenomenal world, but to the world of human values and development. Kierkegaard, on the other hand, urged us to accept by faith alone the paradox of God coming from the noumenal world into our world in human form in the person of Jesus Christ. Both of these responses stress the importance of the decisions and commitments of the *existing individual*, rather than the all-encompassing character of Absolute Spirit.

For his part, Nietzsche limited the concept of transcendence to the evolutionary progression of human character and values in the here and now. As a "transvaluator of values," Nietzsche maintained that the life principle of growth and self-assertion—what he called "the will to power"—is the only viable criterion for evaluating human decisions and behavior. Thus Nietzsche is properly classified as a naturalist as well as an existentialist. Kierkegaard, on the other hand, construed transcendence in terms of the "infinite qualitative distinction between the finite and the infinite." In this mode, God cannot be *known* at all, but only *believed* in by faith. Transcendence is impossible through reason, but possible through faith.

Twentieth-century existentialism continued to develop along these two parallel yet distinctive lines, the naturalistic and the theistic, respectively. Heidegger, Sartre, and Camus each followed more in Nietzsche's tradition, stressing the necessity and difficulty of "authentic existence" in the face of the absurdities and anguish of both life and death, as well as idealism, rationalism, and religion. The "death of God" in our times signals the ultimate irrelevance of the notion of transcendence for modern existence. All that remains, and it is claimed to be more than enough, is for individuals to "accept the benign indifference of the universe" (Camus) and in "honest, good faith" (Sartre) affirm the "Being that lies behind both being(s) and nothingness" (Heidegger). In the midst of the stark chaos of life, the only meaning that remains for human existence is that which we ourselves give to it.

Other existentialist thinkers, notably Gabriel Marcel, Jacques Maritain, and Paul Tillich, have continued in the spirit of Kierkegaard. They acknowledged the absurdity of human existence when approached from the standpoint of either traditional philosophy or religion, while affirming the meaningfulness of the transcendent in relation to existential realities, values, and decisions. The response of faith to the mysteries of life—especially as expressed by philosophy, the arts, and science—is not only possible but uniquely appropriate, since it alone provides a deep and lasting sense of meaning. In this purview, the transcendent remains viable, but only as the "horizon" or "ground" of existence and meaning. It is neither "beyond" this world, à la Plato, nor in this world by way of divine intervention (miracles, etc.). In Kant's terminology, transcendence has taken on a "regulative" function rather than a "substantive" one.

As I mentioned in section one, my own concern is to rethink the notion of transcendence in such a way as to render it more concrete and relevant than the traditional definition will allow, on the one hand, and more rich and comprehensive than a standard naturalism will allow, on the other hand. In like manner, my concern is to integrate the insights of modern scientific thought with the radical integrity of the contemporary existentialist posture. I suggest that both the defenders and the detractors of transcendence have been looking for it in the wrong place. It is time to rethink the notion from the vantage point provided by the concept of mediation.

Two

BEING:

Reality

as Dimensional and Mediated

After one has acknowledged the loss of transcendence, both as a conceptual category and as a viable aspect of religious or ethical life, there are two responses that must be avoided. The first is that of resignation. I hope that the brief sketch of the history of Western thought presented in the introductory chapter made it clear that the notion of transcendence has been lost because of specific tendencies and developments at the ideational level. Thus it can be recovered by retracing our steps and locating the place or places at which a wrong turn was taken. This process is difficult and costly, demanding both imagination and patience on the one hand, and a willingness to acknowledge error on the other.

At the same time it is extremely important not to view this retracing as a return to former, more traditional understandings of transcendence. Not all of the developments in modern thought have been debilitating. It is not the purpose of these reflections to champion a rearguard, reactionary, or romanticist point of view. Indeed, there is much of value in *both* the traditional and the modern perspectives. However, a postmodern perspective seeks to construct a synthesis of these two that will take us beyond them both while preserving their undeniable contributions. Nevertheless, such a synthesis must be Hegelian in the best sense of the term; that is, it must pivot upon an essentially fresh axis, one that simultaneously fulfills, negates, and transcends the previous perspectives.

The area of concern that may serve to provide at least one coordinate for locating this fresh axis is that of Being. We shall begin, then, with an examination of metaphysical and ontological categories by way of suggesting a postmodern vision of reality, its contours and its dynamics. More specifically, we shall begin with a proposal for replacing the model of reality that lies at the center of both traditional and modern thought with a more functional and fruitful model.

1. Realms and Dimensions

The largely unarticulated model of reality around which both traditional and modern thought revolve is one of the realms or spheres located in space and separated by barriers of some kind. In classical and medieval times it was generally assumed that there are *two* or perhaps *three* main realms or "stories" in the cosmic "house," while in modern times it has generally been concluded that there is but *one* sphere within which all reality is contained. The traditional, or vertical, model stresses the contrast between the "here and now" and the "there and then," between appearance and Reality; in short, it is dualistic. The modern, or horizontal, model is defined largely by its denial of any realms but the here and now, as well as by its affirmation of the sufficiency of the principles of this realm to account for the totality of all that happens and all that can be known.

Let us consider the thought of Plato and Kant as representative, if not paradigmatic, of the traditional and modern perspectives, respectively. More specifically, let us take a look at the root metaphors that inform these two dominant systems of thought, as they are revealed in the images that lie at the center of their distinctive projects. I contend that in large measure the whole history of Western thought revolves around the differences inherent in these two equally persuasive, yet equally counterproductive, images, and that both of them presuppose construing reality as made up of realms separated by barriers. First, consider Plato's pivotal passage:

> The prison dwelling corresponds to the region revealed to us through the sense of sight, and the fire-light within it to the power of the Sun. The ascent to see the things in the upper world you may take as standing for the upward journey of the soul into the region of the intelligible; then you will be in possession of what I surmise, since that is what you wish to be told. Heaven knows whether it is true; but this, at any rate, is how it appears to me. In the world of knowledge, the last thing to be perceived and only with great difficulty is the essential Form of Goodness. Once it is perceived, the

conclusion must follow that, for all things, this is the cause of whatever is right and good; in the visible world it gives birth to light and to the lord of light, while it is itself sovereign in the intelligible world and the parent of intelligence and truth.[1]

The driveshaft of Plato's entire enterprise is the distinction between the worlds of becoming and Being, between the worlds of belief and knowledge, as it is imaged in the allegory of the cave and the diagram of the divided line. When these two images are superimposed on each other, the result is a picture of reality in which the "upper world" outside the cave (the "intelligible world") is separated from the "lower world" inside the cave (the world of appearances). This dualistic view of reality places what is eternal and transcendent—the true, the good, and the beautiful—above and essentially beyond the reach of the temporal and fluctuating domain of sensation. The upper story of Plato's world is the realm of the *truly* real, while the lower story is merely a poor reflection of this upper domain.

To be sure, it is to Plato's credit that in his later dialogues, specifically *Parmenides* and *The Sophist,* he acknowledged many difficulties inherent in this worldview and even suggested that the world of becoming is, in its own way, as real as the world of Being. Nevertheless, it was not Plato's later works that established Platonism as the most influential philosophy in Western thought. Moreover, it is the dualism entailed in the imagery of the cave and the divided line that served as the inspiration and blueprint for the construction of the traditional concept of transcendence, especially as it took shape within Christian theology. Not only was the divine placed beyond the human (the supernatural beyond the natural), but the latter was exhaustively explained in terms of the former. In addition, any interaction between these two realms, by means of revelation and/or miracle, was strictly a one-way affair and was construed as an act of intervention by means of which the laws governing the natural were suspended.

Three correlative observations are worth making. One is that within this spatial and "realmistic" view of Plato, the image used to portray knowledge is that of *vision*. Throughout Plato's dialogues, to know is to see. Moreover, cognitive activity—by means of which alone a person can

---

[1]Francis MacDonald Cornford, trans., *The Republic of Plato* (New York: Oxford University Press, 1965) 231.

transcend the domain of appearances—is restricted to the mind, "the eye of the soul." It is interesting to speculate on how the history of Western thought might have been radically different had Plato's root metaphor been that of sound, or touch, or even kinaesthetic awareness *in* space, rather than sight *across* space. Chances are the results would not have been nearly so dualistic.

Also, it is important to note that Plato never actually provides a rationale for his choice of root metaphor in his images of the cave and the divided line. He proposes these images in the context of discussion, and even though they exhibit a great deal of imagination and insight, questions can be raised about their overall helpfulness. The cave image may have been suggested by various Greek mystery religions, while the divided line smacks of Plato's enamorment of geometry. Perhaps these images seemed harmless enough at the time, but from our contemporary perspective one cannot help but wonder whether a less dualistic root metaphor might not have been more helpful.

Finally, there is a certain oneupmanship built into Plato's dualism that leaves it vulnerable to criticism by way of infinite regress. The trouble with basing one's metaphysical theory on the distinction between appearance and reality is that it opens the door for someone else to come along and reclassify what has been called "reality" as merely another form of appearance. Whenever one realm is placed above another, the possibility arises that there may yet be another realm above that, ad infinitum. Such considerations should make us suspicious about the advisability of construing the world according to a realmistic model in the first place.

Plato's two-world view of reality held sway for nearly two thousand years, with only minor modifications contributed by the likes of Aristotle, Augustine, and Aquinas. It was adapted by Christian theologians more because it fit better with Babylonian and Persian influences (which had strong effect in the New Testament world) than because it harmonized with the Hebrew worldview. In fact, Greek dualism stands in direct contradiction to the holistic and organic character of Hebraic understanding. Platonic dualism was challenged by the "horizontalism" of nominalism and empiricism, but it emerged again in slightly different form in the philosophy of Immanuel Kant. While Kant is generally understood to have effected an epistemological version of Plato's dualism, he can also be seen as having developed a modernized version of Plato's dualism, chastened by the analytic critiques of David Hume. Kant's pivotal image is focused thusly:

This domain is an island, enclosed by nature itself within unalterable limits. It is the land of truth—enchanting name!— surrounded by a wide and stormy ocean, the native home of illusion, where many a fog bank and many a swiftly melting iceberg give the deceptive appearance of farther shores, deluding the adventurous seafarer ever anew with empty hopes, and engaging him in enterprises which he can never abandon and yet is unable to carry to completion.[2]

The metaphor by means of which Kant expresses his division of reality into two realms is that of an isolated island surrounded by a sea of meaninglessness. In the midst of his *Critique of Pure Reason,* wherein he delineates the bounds of cognitive activity and thereby renders constructive metaphysics null and void, Kant designates the arena of rational inquiry (the "phenomenal world") as "the island of truth." Only in the domain of formal and natural science can knowledge be pursued and obtained, since the *structure* of the mind determines the way we think by means of the "categories of the understanding" and the "pure intuitions of space and time." Thus at first glance it would appear that Kant had eliminated Plato's world of "pure Being" by denying the possibility of any knowledge thereof (what Kant called "the noumenal world").

The fact is, however, that in his *Critique of Practical Reason,* Kant argued that the central concerns of metaphysics—such questions as the existence of God, the immortality of the soul, and human freedom—are seen to be viable in terms of our moral decisions and judgments. Thus the reality of the metaphysical mainland beyond the fog-banked and iceberg-filled sea is affirmed and established in relation to our *ethical* life, on the basis of what Kant calls "the postulates of practical reason." In contemporary terms, this realm of moral reality is, to be sure, "noncognitive" in the narrow sense of the term, but it remains both real and relevant by virtue of being entailed by our practical rational activity. Questions concerning what we should *do* are every bit as important as questions concerning what we can *know,* according to Kant, and reality is constituted by both. Therefore it is fair to say that what Kant denied in his first critique he affirmed in his second, albeit by way of complementarity rather than contradiction.

The end result, then, is essentially the same as with Platonism. The worlds of becoming and Being are separated, this time by distinguishing

---

[2]Norman Kemp Smith, trans., *Immanuel Kant's Critique of Pure Reason* (New York: St. Martin's Press, 1929) 257.

between *kinds* of rationality (pure and practical), with the questions of cosmic and existential significance serving as our point of access to the realm of the transcendent. The two worlds, the phenomenal and the noumenal, are equally real, but the latter transcends the former in the sense that its reality lies beyond the reach of human reason per se and must be encountered in moral decision making. These two realms are, so to speak, "separate but equal"; nevertheless, the moral life is clearly more fundamental since every person operates therein, while not everyone needs to engage in scientific and/or philosophic activity. Modern dualism is a bit more tolerant and egalitarian than classical dualism, but in the last analysis is pretty much the same.

The contemporary bifurcation between existentialists and phenomenologists on the one hand and logical empiricists and ordinary language philosophers on the other hand clearly reflects the degree to and depth at which this dualism continues to dominate the philosophical and theological scene. This is not to say that these schools of thought are themselves dualistic, but rather that each accepts the general presupposition that reality is and can be divided into two realms. The contemporary disagreements are over which of the two realms is the more important or basic, over whether Kant's first or second *Critique* is the more fundamental. The fact/value split that characterizes our time is a direct result of thinking of reality as dividable into separated realms, regardless of which side of the dichotomy one wishes to emphasize. Thus we continue to be haunted by the ghost of dualism, even in modern and contemporary modes of thought.

Over against this realmistic way of construing reality I would propose a *dimensional* model. The basic difference lies in understanding reality as composed of a number of simultaneously interpenetrating dimensions rather than as separate levels or domains. Moreover, these dimensions are experienced as *mediated* in and through one another rather than being juxtaposed to each other. In contrast to Plato's dualistic image of the cave and Kant's image of the boundary between the phenomenal and the noumenal, consider William James's pivotal image in the following passage from his lectures on pragmatism:

> I have sometimes thought of the phenomenon called "total reflexion" in Optics as a good symbol of the relation between abstract ideas and concrete realities, as pragmatism conceives it. Hold a tumbler of water a little above your eyes and look up through the water at its surface—or better still look similarly through the flat wall of an aquarium. You will then see

an extraordinarily brilliant reflected image say of a candle-flame, or any other clear object, situated on the opposite side of the vessel. No ray, under these circumstances gets beyond the water's surface: every ray is totally reflected back into the depths again. Now let the water represent the world of sensible facts, and let the air above it represent the world of abstract ideas. Both worlds are real, of course, and interact; but they interact only at their boundary, and the *locus* of everything that lives, and happens to us, so far as full experience goes, is the water. We are like fishes swimming in the sea of sense, bounded above by the superior element, but unable to breathe it pure or penetrate it. We get our oxygen from it, however, we touch it incessantly, now in this part, now in that, and every time we touch it, we turn back into the water with our course re-determined and re-energized. The abstract ideas of which the air consists are indispensable for life, but irrespirable by themselves, as it were, and only active in their re-directing function. All similes are halting, but this one rather takes my fancy. It shows how something, not sufficient for life itself, may nevertheless be an effective determinant of life elsewhere.[3]

What James is talking about is the relationship between tangible and intangible reality, the same general concern of Plato and Kant, as well as of others who have followed in their footsteps. His particular focus is on abstract ideas and physical objects; with Kant he is saying that they (percepts and concepts) each need each other, albeit in different ways. He also speaks, as Kant does, of the boundary between them. What is crucial to notice, however, is that the dynamics of the processes involved in James's image are quite distinct from those of Kant, as well as from those of Plato. For the light rays are experienced exclusively in and through the glass and the water while nevertheless being distinct from them. For the fish, it makes no sense to conceive of the light source as independent of the rays diffused by and through the water. At the same time, however, it cannot be construed as merely the sum total of the physical realities through which it is mediated.

In James's image, the intangible reality is not a realm existing beyond the tangible water enclosed in the aquarium. Rather, it is the light that diffuses itself throughout the water while still not being equatable with it. The two are logically distinct, yet without being separable from each other in the totality of the viewer's experience; nor can they be neatly compartmentalized, à la Kant. What we have here is a worldview similar

---

[3]William James, *Pragmatism* (New York: Longmans, Green and Co., 1925) 127-28.

to that of Aristotle when he insisted that form and matter cannot be separated. I am urging a revitalization of this dimensional and mediational model as a way of overcoming the dualism, together with its resultant stalemate, that both dominates and undermines our contemporary thinking with respect to the notion of transcendence.

Permit me both to extend and emend James's image a bit in order to clarify further the difference between a realmistic and a dimensional way of construing reality. Consider the dynamics involved in the transmission of oxygen from the air to the bloodstream of the fish in a water tank. Clearly, the fish needs oxygen in order to live, yet when removed from the tank it is unable to obtain what it needs from the surrounding air. Indeed, things would be no better were the fish placed in an environment of pure oxygen. Instead, the oxygen in the air must be processed in and through the water and the fish's gill system in order for it to be *real* to the fish. Both the oxygen and the water are experienced by the fish, the former in and through the latter; both constitute essential dimensions of the fish's reality, but they interpenetrate each other.

My overall point is simply that our existence in space is dimensional, not realmistic. When we move in space we do so in three dimensions *at once*, not from one compartment to another. Thus a dimensional model of existence and experience is more fitting than a realmistic one. Moreover, some of the dimensions of experienced reality are encountered in and through the others as in a superimposure or an alteration of musical key. The more intangible dimensions of reality are nonetheless real for being mediated through the more tangible. This is a common feature of our everyday lives. Attitudes and intentions are expressed and discerned in and through glances, intonations, and even silences. Momentum and team spirit in an athletic contest are experienced as realities by means of various tangible factors, but few would claim that the former are reducible to the latter. It is this same pattern of dimensional mediation that I am proposing as a more fruitful way to think of the structure of our existence, as a more helpful model of how we experience reality.

Let me now bring these considerations to bear on the question of transcendence. When the realmistic model is used as the basis for our thinking of the transcendent—as has been the case throughout the history of most Western thought—the result is that the transcendent realm, whether Plato's Forms or God's cosmic rule, is placed "above" and construed as essentially independent of the natural or empirical realm. This is necessary, it is generally claimed, in order to preserve the qualitative *superiority* and ontological *priority* of that which is most fundamentally real. However, once this independence is established, it becomes very difficult to establish any organic and meaningful point of connection between the two realms. Plato acknowledges this difficulty in his later dialogue, *The Sophist*, and Kant sought to alleviate it by means of the "postulates of practical reason." Neither of these concessionary moves actually resolved the difficulty, however; they only focused it more sharply by attempting to ignore the implications of their basic initial commitments.

When all of this is cast in a theological mode, the focus of the difficulty is generally the concept of revelation or divine agency in the world. If the divine reality is said to be "above" and independent of our world, how then can God be said to act in the world? In addition, if God's ways are absolutely "not our ways," then how can we ever know anything about God and the divine intentions? The traditional concept of divine transcendence, to be sure, affirms the complementary immanence of God as well, but it is never made clear how these two are interrelated on the basis of a realmistic model. Either God is *beyond* the world and cannot be known or spoken about, or God is active *in* the world and this activity can be recognized on the basis of the same criteria by which we acknowledge the reality of other agencies. If the criteria are said to be "special"—that is, transcendent—then we are back to square one again, since we have no criteria by means of which to recognize transcendent criteria.

The notion of mediated dimensions speaks to this dualistic difficulty by affirming the reality of a transcendent dimension that exists and is known in and through the natural dimension or dimensions of human existence. This transcendent reality is nevertheless more or other than that through which it is mediated, yet without being independent of it. Thus God can be said to exist and be revealed in and through the world without being beyond and independent of it.

2. Hierarchies and Boundaries

Much has been made recently, and rightly so, of the notions of context and horizon. Among linguistic philosophers, following the lead of Wittgenstein, the importance of *context* in determining meaning has become paramount. The use to which a given utterance is put in a specific context is the very matrix of linguistic meaning. Moreover, a given use may also be governed by a broader context, namely by what Wittgenstein termed the "language-game" within which it functions. This suggests a hierarchy of contexts leading all the way back to our human way-of-being-in-the-world, our "form of life." In like manner, among phenomenologists the notion of horizon is employed in order to indicate the relationship between the outer limits of our situation and the point in space and time at which we stand. Wherever and whenever we are, we are bounded by the horizon, even though as our existential situation shifts our horizon shifts with it. The relationship between ourselves and our horizon remains constant, and yet each ensuing horizon incorporates the previous ones. This, too, suggests a hierarchy of horizons, each more comprehensive than the last.

It is this sort of hierarchical pattern that characterizes our experience of reality as dimensional. Not only do the various dimensions of reality interpenetrate and mediate one another, but they are arranged in a mediational hierarchy according to their varying degrees of richness and comprehensiveness. The level of meaning of any given dimension emerges out of those levels that ground and mediate it in such a manner as to both depend upon and transcend them. For example, the meaning of this sentence I am now writing emerges out of, yet goes beyond, the central features of such other linguistic dimensions as grammatical structure, lexical definitions, phonemes, and cursive symbols.

In his important book *Faith and Knowledge,* John Hick develops this notion of mediational hierarchy in a most interesting fashion. Here is a helpful passage from his presentation in which he discusses three such dimensions: the natural, the ethical, and the religious.

> Clearly, moral significance presupposes natural significance. For in order that we may be conscious of moral obligations, and exercise moral intelligence, we must first be aware of a stable environment in which actions have foreseeable results, and in which we can learn the likely consequences of our deeds. It is thus a precondition of ethical situations that there should be a stable medium, the world, with its own causal laws, in which people meet and in terms of which they act. The two spheres of significance, the moral and the physical, interpenetrate in the sense that all occasions of obligation have reference, either immediately or ultimately, to overt action. Relating oneself to the ethical sphere is thus a particular manner of relating oneself to the natural sphere; ethical significance is mediated to us in and through the natural world. . . . As ethical significance interpenetrates natural significance, so religious significance interpenetrates both ethical and natural. The divine is the highest and ultimate order of significance, mediating neither of the others and yet being mediated through both of them. . . . Thus the primary religious perception, or basic act of religious interpretation, is not to be described as either a reasoned conclusion or an unreasoned hunch that there is a God. It is, putatively, an apprehension

of the divine presence within the believer's human experience. It is not an inference to a general truth, but a "divine-human encounter," a mediated meeting with the living God.[4]

The particular ins and outs and overall value of Hick's specific application of this dimensional and mediational model are not at issue at this juncture. I am simply borrowing his central notion as a deeply insightful and helpful one for reconstructing the notion of transcendence in our contemporary situation. This model provides us a way to retain transcendence as a viable concept, thus avoiding the liabilities of reductionism, without resorting to traditional dualism, thus avoiding the shortcomings of metaphysical "reactionary-ism." Let's explore the hierarchical character of this model in more detail.

It is difficult but unnecessary to specify how many dimensions constitute our experienced reality. We may want to include the aesthetic and the personal as well as the social, along with the natural, the moral, and the religious. It is the pattern that is of interest and value, not the specific number of dimensions. The main point is that in a general way the dimensions making up our world can be arranged according to a mediational hierarchy on the basis of their varying degrees of *richness* and *comprehensiveness*. That is, they can be seen as enfolding into one another as parts of a collapsible telescope; each arises out of and yet is contained within each successively larger part.

To employ one of Hick's examples, consider the differences in levels of significance resulting from an encounter with a message written on a piece of paper by (1) a person who knows *nothing* about written languages, (2) a person who knows *about* them but who does not know any, (3) a person who knows written languages but not *this* one, and (4) a person who can actually *read* the message in question. Clearly, each person experiences something quite different when confronted with the message, yet each experiences exactly the same physical phenomena. Progressing from the first person to the last, it is correct to say that each level of significance is mediated in and through the previous level, that it is at once the same as and more than the previous level.

The resolution of this paradoxical way of speaking, of course, lies in acknowledging that at each progressive level there exists an increase of

---

[4]John Hick, *Faith and Knowledge*, 2d ed. (Ithaca NY: Cornell University Press, 1966) 112, 113, 115.

richness and complexity on one hand, as well as an increased inclusive-ness on the other hand. Each successive level incorporates and goes be-yond the previous ones, while arising out of and being dependent on them. Thus there is no message apart from grammar and vocabulary, no words without written symbols, and so on. What we have here is a hi-erarchy of mediated dimensions that emerge out of each other according to a pattern of increased complexity and significance (which I have termed "richness"), as well as wider and wider inclusiveness (which I have termed "comprehensiveness").

Consider yet another example. Three persons are standing on a bridge watching a group of swimmers. Suddenly they see a small child floating face down in the current. One person says, "There's eighty-five pounds of protoplasm floating in a mixture of H_2O and moving south by southeast at a rate of one mile an hour." A second person says, "Notice the contrast of colors between the child's body and the water surface as both the wind and the sunlight play upon them amidst the twirling of the current." The third person says, "My God, it's a child drowning! We have a duty to save it." Now, each of these successive descriptions is *inclusive* of the previous one(s) and thus is neither in conflict with nor ultimately independent of them, while at the same time each *transcends* the others in the sense of going beyond them to provide a broader perspective. In short, each is richer and more comprehensive in that its contextual understanding and horizon is deeper and more inclusive.

In this example, the three persons involved are not, at one level, dis-agreeing with each other. The purely physical description is entirely cor-rect, *as far as it goes.* The aesthetic description, which both depends upon the physical dimension and goes beyond it, does not negate it. In like manner, the moral description is mediated in and through the other di-mensions—or at least does not deny the aesthetic—but yet it transcends them by providing a perspective that the vast majority of human beings would acknowledge as more significant and encompassing. Thus we have here a hierarchy of dimensions of experience or significance arranged ac-cording to increased richness and comprehensiveness.

My suggestion is that this same familiar pattern can be employed as a means of understanding how a transcendent or divine dimension of real-ity might be active in human experience without being reducible to the other dimensions constituting that experience. Had there been a fourth, a religious, person on the bridge, she might have said something like the fol-lowing: "In and through the dimensions of which the rest of you speak I discern a reality at work which enables me more deeply to appreciate and integrate these other dimensions. I call it 'God.' " The question of how we determine which and how many dimensions to legitimize will have to be postponed until the next chapter. Here I am concerned to show how our experienced reality is fruitfully understood as a hierarchy of mediated dimensions and how such understanding establishes (or reestablishes) the viability of the notion of transcendence for a contemporary understanding of ontology. For it provides a way of avoiding the pitfalls of both traditional dualism and modern reductionism, as well as the stalemate that has resulted from their mutual confrontation.

Before moving on, perhaps a further word or two would be in order about the meaning of the terms *richness* and *comprehensiveness*, especially as they are applied to the religious dimension of existence. It seems intuitively clear that the aesthetic and moral dimensions of experienced reality, as well as of the personal and social, are richer and more comprehensive than the physical dimension. The same would seem to hold true for the moral dimension in relation to each of the others, since the moral quality of our existence almost always is given precedence over the others. It is *richer* in that it is both more complex and more important. It is more *comprehensive* in that it encompasses the others without being encompassed by them. Moral awareness is thus said to be the highest level of human life because it is regarded as the fundamentally most significant.

The same can be said, it seems to me, about the religious or divine dimension of experienced reality. Nearly all, if not in fact all, peoples have incorporated some version of this transcendent dimension into their behavior and belief systems. Moreover, this dimension of human existence is universally deemed the controlling one, the one that gives order and meaning to the others. The economy, the mores, the institutions, and the art of almost all cultures—the primal to the most technologically sophisticated—are said to derive their significance from the overarching mythological structure within which they operate. Thus the religious dimension of human experience, for good or for ill, can be said to provide the deepest and widest context or horizon for understanding the world as we know it.

It will prove helpful to examine further the interrelationships between and among the various dimensions forming the hierarchical structure of our mediational experience of reality. As I have already indicated, there exists an asymmetrical or *vectorial* relationship between those dimensions that are mediated and those by which they are mediated. In other words, the former not only include and rely upon the latter, but in a sense they are controlled by them as well. Even as the physical dimension of existence both gives rise to and is transcended by the moral dimension, it also sets the *boundary conditions* for the latter. Whatever shape and development our moral considerations take, they are necessarily grounded in and limited to persons as embodied agents. Our moral judgments and decisions, in other words, must always pertain to what people do and say in their behavioral interactions with one another. Morality, in short, is bounded by the physical world, although it is not exhausted by it.

The mistake of traditional dualists, from Plato to contemporary representatives, is to insist that morality, as well as the divine, exists independently of the physical world. This renders it "so heavenly-minded as to be of no earthly good." In their enthusiasm to safeguard the importance of the transcendent, such thinkers—both philosophical and theological—failed to ground it in the physical, thereby making it ethereal and irrelevant. The same holds true for the traditional ways in which God is said to be related to the world. Both theism and pantheism founder because they assume that one must choose between divine transcendence and immanence. Both fail to consider the possibility of mediating dimensions of reality that are arranged asymmetrically in a hierarchy of significance, with the physical both setting the minimal boundary conditions and providing the mediational matrix for the divine.

The mistake of modern reductionists, from Hobbes to Skinner, is to conclude that since the personal and the moral dimensions of life, as well as the religious, must be grounded in and are limited by the physical dimension, the former are nothing but complex manifestations of the latter. In their enthusiasm to rid modern understanding of metaphysical charades and "ghosts in the machines," modern reductionists (including those in theology) have failed to notice that not only have they made human existence one-dimensional and less significant, but they have overlooked a fundamental characteristic of experienced reality in the process. The characteristic I have in mind is what Michael Polanyi has called "emergence," the capacity for less complex forms of reality to give rise to more complex forms that are in fact irreducible to the former. Thus inanimate reality yields animate reality and biological existence yields consciousness. In spite of all their claims and promises, reductionists remain unable to explain one form of life strictly in terms of another, less complex form. The concept of explanation itself is a phenomenon that pertains to *minds* but not to brains.

At this point let me quote a rather lengthy passage from Polanyi that delineates the relationship between lower-level boundary conditions and the higher principles that govern their use.

Next we recognize that in certain cases the boundary conditions of a principle are in fact subject to control by other principles. These I will call higher principles. Thus the boundary conditions of the laws of mechanics may be controlled by the operational principles which define a machine, the boundary conditions of muscular action may be controlled by a pattern of purposive behaviour, like that of going for a walk; the boundary conditions of a vocabulary are usually controlled by the rules of grammar, and the conditions left open by the rules of chess are controlled by the stratagems of the players. And so we find that machines, purposive actions, grammatical sentences, and games of chess, are all entities subject to *dual control*.

Such is the stratified structure of comprehensive entities. They embody a combination of two principles, a higher and a lower. Smash up a machine, utter words at random, or make chess moves without a purpose, and the corresponding higher principle—that which constitutes the machine, that which makes words in sentences, and that which makes moves of chess into a game—will all vanish and the comprehensive entity which they controlled will cease to exist.

But the lower principles, the boundary conditions of which the now effaced higher principles had controlled, remain in operation. The laws of mechanics, the vocabulary sanctioned by the dictionary, the rules of chess, they will all continue to apply as before. Hence no description of a comprehensive entity in the light of its lower principles can ever reveal the operation of its higher principles. *The higher principles which characterize a comprehensive entity cannot be defined in terms of the laws that apply to its parts in themselves.*[5]

A slightly different way to come at this interaction between boundary conditions and controlling principles is in terms of Gestalt perception theory. The central idea here is that instead of perception being simply a function of the gradual buildup of the particular sensations we receive, it is rather better understood in the reverse order. First we perceive meaningful wholes, or what Polanyi terms "comprehensive entities," and then we are able to analyze them in terms of their constituent particulars. As infants, to be sure, much of our sensory intake is random and atomized, although recent research in this area indicates that it is much less so than has been traditionally thought. Nevertheless, at the level of significance it is with *wholes* that we have to do, not with parts.

---

[5]Michael Polanyi, *Knowing and Being* (Chicago: University of Chicago Press, 1969) 217.

Although our initial sensory "exposures" seem to be to the particular data that form the parts of the meaningful wholes that we eventually come to grasp, the fact is that these particulars are not cognized *as* parts of anything at all until *after* the whole in question is grasped. In the process of repeated exposure, something happens that transforms simple stimuli into meaningful wholes, and this something cannot be explained simply in terms of repeated exposure to particulars. This capacity of the mind to transform sensation into cognition exemplifies the principles governing the relationship between boundary conditions and higher principles of significance. The former set the parameters for the latter, but the latter constitute the meaning of the former. The one is the sine qua non and the other the raison d'être of the hierarchical structure of reality. Here is Polanyi's application of this asymmetrical analysis to linguistic activity:

> The theory of boundary conditions recognized the higher levels of life as forming a hierarchy, each level of which relies for its workings on the principles of the levels below it, even while it itself is irreducible to these lower principles. I shall illustrate the structure of such a hierarchy by showing the way five levels make up a spoken literary composition.
>
> The lowest level is the production of a voice; the second, the utterance of word; the third, the joining of words to make sentences; the fourth, the working of sentences into a style; the fifth, and highest, the compositions of the text.
>
> The principles of each level operate under the control of the next higher level. The voice you produce is shaped into words by a vocabulary; a given vocabulary is shaped into sentences in accordance with a grammar; and the sentences are fitted into a style, which in its turn is made to convey the ideas of the composition. Thus each level is subject to dual control: (i) control in accordance with the laws that apply to its elements in themselves, and (ii) control in accordance with the laws of the powers that control the comprehensive entity formed by these elements.[6]

Let me offer two examples in contemporary thought wherein the reality of emergence and dual control are left out. The first is Marxism. For all of his penetrating and original analysis of the human situation, Marx's contention that social and cultural life (the "superstructure") are entirely a function of economic life (the "substructure") simply will not hold up. Many, if not most people, and indeed some cultures as well, are fre-

---

[6]Ibid., 233.

quently prepared to limit or modify the nature of their economic existence in accord with certain social or moral values. This is clearly the case
with respect to religious values and beliefs. Surely, the economic level is
necessary to sustain the moral and/or religious level, but it is anything but
sufficient to explain it. Neither is more important than the other, since
both are crucial, but the one (the means) exists *for* the other (the end) and
not vice versa. Marx himself, as well as the overall thrust of his philosophy, surely substantiates this.

Second, consider the insightful and influential theories of psycholo-
gist Abraham Maslow. His analysis of the hierarchy of human values, from
what he termed "deficiency needs" to "self-actualizing needs," tends to
imply that until one has fulfilled the former one cannot go forward to the
latter. This idea is often encountered in folk-wisdom adages such as: "You
can't worry about freedom when your stomach is empty" and "People in
chains have no time for religion." But clearly, the very opposite is true.
Frequently the most destitute and oppressed people are the most concerned about politics and religion. The aborigines of the Australian out-
back used to spend most of their waking hours grubbing for roots to eat,
yet they developed extremely complex rituals and religious beliefs. Here
again, there is a failure to distinguish between means and ends. Just because subsistence needs constitute the necessary parameters of existence, it does not follow that they constitute the bottom line. Some things
are more important than life itself; in fact, it is such things that make life
worth living.

Now to return to the main theme of our discussion: my proposal is
that human experience is best seen as structured according to a hierarchy
of mediated dimensions arranged according to richness and comprehensiveness. Moreover, this hierarchy functions according to a pattern of
"dual control" provided by the boundary conditions set by the less rich
and comprehensive dimensions on the one hand and the higher principles of the richer and more comprehensive dimensions on the other
hand. The meaning of the higher dimensions is mediated in and through
that of the lower dimensions in such a way that the former is dependent
upon the latter without being reducible to it.

The overall purpose of this proposal is, of course, to provide a means
of reclaiming the notion of transcendence for our time without falling back
into traditional dualistic ways of thinking and speaking. It is my conviction that this model of mediated dimensions arranged in a hierarchy of
richness and comprehensiveness allows us to conceive of transcendence
in the manner suggested. It is now time to explore more thoroughly the

notion of mediation as a way of clarifying the dynamics involved in the interaction among the various dimensions of experienced reality.

3. Mediation and Significance

Having delineated the structure of experienced reality in terms of a hierarchy of dimensions, it is appropriate to take a closer look at the dynamics of the mediational process by means of which the various dimensions interact and communicate significance. The axis of this process is the disclosure of reality and meaning *in and through* the particular components and aspects of the mediating dimension. Just how does this take place?

Perhaps the most helpful way to begin is with some concrete cases in point. The mediational process is in no way mysterious or magical, unless all of life is to be so designated, since the process is exceedingly commonplace. Indeed, nearly every level of human life revolves around and flows from this process in some form or other. Because we have become so enamored of the processes of objectification and inferential reasoning, we generally lose sight of the role mediational understanding plays in cognition, even with respect to the two processes just mentioned. Consider some examples.

Let's begin with aesthetic awareness. We often encounter motion, say, in a painting or sadness in a piece of music. Now, in terms of the tangible qualities of the painting or music, it makes little sense to look or listen for motion or sadness in them. A painting is made up of color, shape, line, and space, or of chemicals, canvas, and the like, and thus cannot be said to contain or exhibit motion per se. In like manner, a piece of music is made up of sounds, silences, pitches, and rhythm, or of notes, time, and key, but sadness is not a musical quality as such. Nevertheless, we do experience these intangible qualities when interacting with various works of art. How shall we explain this phenomenon?

Some, to be sure, would explain it strictly in terms of the illusory character of art. Others would reduce it to a form of operant conditioning arising from the correlation of certain perceptual data and certain emotions. Still others would simply say that such qualities are strictly in "the eye of the beholder," possessing a merely subjective value. Clearly, these are all important factors, helpful as far as they go. However, they do not explain our experience of such qualities *as experienced*. For each of the above explanations is a post facto, and thus ad hoc, treatment of the reality of intangible qualities as encountered in everyday life. *After* we find ourselves experiencing our world as one in which intangible realities are inextricably intertwined within and by means of tangible realities, it will hardly do to treat the former as if they were ancillary and optional.

From my perspective, it seems far more helpful to say that the dimension of experienced reality that we term the "aesthetic" is encountered in and through the physical dimension, that it is *mediated* by it. This aesthetic dimension is nonetheless real for not being reducible to those factors constituting the dimension through which it is mediated. The latter provides the matrix out of which the former arises; the particular configuration of factors constituting the less rich dimension gives rise to but does not *entail* the richer, more comprehensive dimension. Motion and sadness are reasonably said to be *in* the painting or piece of music, respectively, without being isolatable from the sensory particulars thereof.

This mediational process is not a passive encounter in which the intangible is pressed into our awareness in absentia. An integral feature of the mediational process is the interaction between the knowing subject and that which is known. Intangible realities, such as those constituting the aesthetic dimension of experienced reality, are only encountered when and as one participates in them. There is a kind of empathetic understanding—what some have called *Verstehen*—involved in this type of awareness. The following remarks, especially the final one, exemplify Wittgenstein's insight into this mediational process.

It seems paradoxical to us that we should make such a medley, mixing physical states and states of consciousness up together in a single report: "He suffered great torments and tossed about restlessly." It is quite usual; so why do we find it paradoxical? Because we want to say that the sentence deals with both tangibles and intangibles at once.—But does it worry you if I say: "These three struts give the building stability?" Are three and stability tangible?—Look at the sentence as an instrument, and at its sense as its employment. . . . It is possible to say "I read timidity in this face" but at all events the timidity does not seem to be merely associated, outwardly connected, with the face; but fear is there, alive, in the features. If the features change slightly, we can speak of a corresponding change in the fear. "I noticed that he was out of humour." Is this a report about his behavior or his state of mind? ("The sky looks threatening": is this about the present or the future?) Both; not side-by-side, however, but about the one via the other.

Do I really see something different each time, or do I only interpret what I see in a different way? I am inclined to say the former. But why?—To interpret is to think, to do something; seeing is a state.[7]

Consider, as another example, the phenomenon of language acquisition. While some, following Skinner, would have us believe that verbal behavior is simply a function of repeated exposure to certain reinforcement patterns, and others, following Chomsky, explain it all in terms of the innate structure of the brain, there remain far too many unanswered questions to grant either of these approaches viability as total explanations. Chomsky has shown that the behaviorist account fails to explain a child's ability to understand and create speech patterns that have not been previously encountered; and Chomsky's own rationalist approach is essentially a kind of "self-sealer" in the sense that the brain is said to be structured in whatever way necessary to explain the phenomenon of language acquisition.

What is needed here is some notion of the dynamic that enables a child to grasp the intangible meanings mediated by the tangible sounds and patterns of everyday speech. Clearly something more is called for than repeated exposures, but the "more" that is required must be disclosed and discerned *within* such exposures, not prior to and independent of them. The key lies in the child's being drawn into the warp and weft of human activity and speech, which in turn gives rise to interaction with the "meanings" expressed in human language. This latter dimension is mediated in and through the former by means of the structure of the *human form of life* as a whole, not just the layout of the brain.

A parallel example can be found in our awareness of other persons. The personal and/or social dimension of experienced reality can helpfully be said to be mediated to us in and through our interaction with the bodily behavior of others. From the very beginning—if not before—we are spoken to and touched by others, and when and as we respond in kind we are aware of their reality as persons. Only philosophers first posit self-knowledge and then wonder how we can avoid skepticism about others. As persons participating in a common life form, we experience others as real from the outset. If anything, we are aware of others before we become aware of ourselves. The crucial point is to recognize that this aware-

---

[7]Ludwig Wittgenstein, *Philosophical Investigations* (New York: Macmillan Company, 1953) 212.

ness of other persons is mediated in and through their behavior. It is neither intuited nor inferred; rather, it arises out of the push-and-pull, the give-and-take of everyday experience. Such awareness of the personal and/or social dimension is not available apart from the behavioral particulars, but neither can it be reduced to an account of them.

Once again the pivotal dynamic of this mediational awareness is interaction. The intangible dimensions of reality can only be discerned by those who "gear into" them, who join the dance or play the game. Some sort of participation, whether empathetic or active, is required for knowledge of persons, as is the case with all forms of intangible reality. When and because we are addressed and treated as persons, as those who will understand and respond, we in turn address and treat others as persons. Thereby we participate in and exemplify the intangible reality of personhood. Behavior mediates this reality but does not exhaust it. Furthermore, such realities are only mediated to those who embody or indwell them at the interactive level. There is nothing esoteric or mystical about this; it is simply the nature of intangible reality to be relational in character.

One way to summarize the main themes of the forgoing discussion is in terms of the notions of disclosure and discernment. *Disclosure* signifies the "objective" pole of the mediational dynamic. Intangible dimensions are disclosed to us as we encounter and interact with them in and through the tangible particulars that both give rise to and find their meaning in them. Such realities as the aesthetic, the linguistic, and the personal dimensions of human existence are disclosed in this mediational manner. They come to us as objectively real; we do not hypothesize or infer them. To put it differently, these sorts of intangible dimensions provide the backdrop or framework within which we operate as active agents, and as such their reality is never in question.

The "subjective" correlate of disclosure is *discernment*. Intangible dimensions of reality do not just float on the surface; they require a degree of commitment and discipline in order to be experienced. Aesthetic qualities are not available to the "innocent eye," only to the "educated eye." If a child is never immersed in language, spoken to and invited to speak back, he or she will never know linguistic reality. Helen Keller's struggle to discern the meaning of Annie Sullivan's "finger-game" enabled her to encounter a multitude of dimensions of reality that previously lay just beyond her grasp. It is through participation and interaction that we come to know intangible dimensions; our discernment grows out of such engagement, and what we discern can also be said to be disclosed to us therein. Mediated meaning is read *in* the particulars of the mediating dimensions. It is neither read *off* of these particulars nor read *into* them.

By now I would hope the significance of all this for the notion of transcendence, especially with reference to metaphysical and ontological questions, has become clear. In each of the cases discussed above, the mediational pattern and process had been seen as central to our awareness of what is real. Intangible dimensions of reality are discerned and disclosed as transcendent to, yet immanent within tangible dimensions. The concept of mediation makes possible the integration of these two traditionally opposed notions. The transcendent is now construed as both within *and* beyond the immanent, as mediated in and through it. This focus on the mediational process at the heart of our awareness of intangible reality allows us to avoid the difficulties of traditional dualism without falling victim to the shortcomings of modern reductionism.

The special significance of this way of conceiving of transcendence for religious and theological reflection is considerable. Specifically, this way of thinking is both informed by and conducive to a truly incarnational model of God's activity in the world. Far too often incarnation has been interpreted in dualistic fashion, with the Logos coming down from the divine realm for a brief visit and then returning to its proper "home" in the sky. Just as unfortunate, however, are those modern interpretations that confine the Logos exclusively to the human realm. A mediational understanding of transcendence allows for, even requires, the disclosure and discernment of the divine in and through the human, thereby negating the traditional, dualistic version as well as flat, humanistic versions. As the New Testament puts it: "The Word *became* flesh and dwelt among us" (John's Gospel) and "God was *in* Christ" (Paul's letter to the Corinthians). More pointedly yet, Paul states: "Now we see through a glass, darkly." Such passages as these harmonize well with a mediational understanding of the relationship between the transcendent and the world of everyday experience.

All of these themes are very cleverly and profoundly put in Edwin Abbott's little book *Flatland*.[8] Written more than a hundred years ago by a British schoolmaster trained in Shakespeare and mathematics, this book explores the dynamics and difficulties of thinking and speaking about dimensions that transcend those to which we are accustomed and confined. Part one provides an account of the culture and morality of a two-

---

[8]Edwin A. Abbott, *Flatland* (New York: Dover Publications, 1952).

dimensional society called Flatland, while part two deals with the adventures of a Flatlander who is first visited by a person from Sphereland and then travels to the third dimension himself, finally returning to his own world.

When the person from Sphereland first confronts the Flatlander, the latter is confused and extremely skeptical of the idea of a dimension of reality that transcends the two dimensions with which he is familiar. Abbott's productive insight in this encounter lies in his use of the notion of dimensions rather than realms. During his visit the Spherelander does not exist in or appear as arriving from a world that is entirely separate from Flatland. Rather, he exists and is experienced in and through the two-dimensional worlds as a person from an *additional* but not separate third dimension. The dimensional model employed by Abbot enables his characters to interact with each other while experiencing their worlds differently. The third dimension transcends yet interpenetrates the two dimensions of Flatland. The former is richer and more comprehensive than the latter, while at the same time incorporating it.

Abbott's Flatlander is somewhat prepared for his encounter with the visitor from Sphereland by some dreams he has of traveling to "Pointland" and "Lineland." Here his own reality is called into question because he transcends the dimensional structures of these worlds without being entirely outside them. He is able to communicate with the inhabitants in a limited way, even though he is unable to convince them of his two-dimensionality. In the same way, when the visitor from Sphereland confronts the Flatlander, the latter has difficulty accepting and comprehending the reality of a dimensionality that transcends his own. Nevertheless, by means of various conceptual innovations and experiential alterations, the Flatlander is brought to recognize and acknowledge the actuality of the third dimension.

The disclosure-discernment pattern operative in these multidimensional interactions is especially interesting in light of our discussion of the mediational process. In lieu of being able to provide objective evidence or rational proof of the transcendent dimension, Abbott's travelers seek either to call attention to paradoxical aspects of the familiar dimensions or to invite their interlocutor to construe the entire world from a completely different perspective. New terminology is introduced, building on but altering traditional usage, and certain perceptual exercises are encouraged. The hope is that such activity will trigger a shift in Gestalt, an awareness of something that is more than the ordinary without being entirely other. These activities, then, serve as the catalyst for the mediation of transcendent significance in and through the everyday.

Perhaps some parallel situations from other dimensions of ordinary experience will shed some light here. When we are trying to help another person understand and appreciate, indeed to experience, a complex activity or phenomenon with which he is unfamiliar, we frequently resort to similar procedures. In the field of aesthetics, for example, metaphors from other media are employed to illuminate some aspect of a given medium, certain perceptual "tricks" are taught (such as blurring one's vision in order to see composition rather than objects), and specific exercises are developed (such as gesture and contour drawing). In sports, to take another example, certain metaphors and expressions may be used, such as "momentum" and "backdoor," or special diagrams and exercises may be created. Two people listening to a symphony or watching a ball game may be used to experience the same thing and two completely different things at one and the same time.

There is, of course, no guarantee that a person will be able to experience the dimension of reality to which another person seeks to introduce him. Mediated significance is not necessarily replicable, nor is it susceptible to an exhaustive account of its components. Seeing an aspect, hearing an insinuation, feeling a mood are all as common as they are difficult to explain. This is because they are patterns of significance that participate in the mediational mode, just as Abbott's dimensional realities do. They can only be located or discerned within the less rich and less comprehensive dimensions of experience, yet they can reasonably be said to transcend them as well. Any account of such phenomena must proceed according to what Clifford Geertz calls "thick description," which is grounded in an empathetic and participatory understanding of the contextual and mediational aspects constituting them.

One, if not the chief difficulty arising in connection with any discussion of the mediational process pertains to the impossibility of identifying that which is being mediated. For, it is of the very essence of such mediational realities not to be isolatable from those factors by which they are mediated. If one assumes that all that is real must be capable of being differentiated from that by means of which it is experienced, nothing much can be said or done by way of establishing the possibility and/or actuality of dimensions that transcend the perceptual. It remains unclear, however, what rationale can be given for this assumption, since the structure and dynamic of everyday experience would seem flatly to contradict such reductionism.

The answer to the question "How many realities are we going to allow in our world?" is, of course, "As many as are necessary and/or useful." The law of parsimony ("Do not multiply entities beyond necessity") must not be interpreted and applied in a strictly one-dimensional manner. In addition to chairs, tables, plants, rocks, and cats, such "things" as numbers, groups, mistakes, friendship, ideas, and seriousness also are real. Furthermore, as I have endeavored to indicate, aesthetic and moral qualities, as well as the personal and religious, are nonetheless real for being mediational in character. Another way to put this is to say that these dimensions of human experience play a crucial part in our lives and as yet have not been explained on the basis of strictly physical principles. The burden of proof for the possibility of such a reductionist account rests with those who would affirm it, not with those who would deny it.

A helpful perspective on this whole ontological question is provided by Nelson Goodman in his book *Ways of Worldmaking*. Therein he argues both creatively and cogently that we all participate in a large number of worlds that are constituted by our shared activity, both linguistic and nonlinguistic. We have as many worlds, or dimensions, and aspects thereof as we collectively find meaningful. None of these worlds, according to Goodman, is more basic or important than any other, in and of themselves. My own view is that while this is essentially true, some are richer and more comprehensive, and are properly said to be mediated in and through the less rich and comprehensive worlds or dimensions. The crucial point for this immediate context, however, is made by Goodman in the following fashion:

> If I ask about the world, you can offer to tell me how it is under one or more frames of reference; but if I insist that you tell me how it is apart from all frames, what can you say? We are confined to ways of describing whatever is described. Our universe, so to speak, consists of these ways rather than a world or of worlds.
>
> What I have said so far plainly points to a radical relativism; but severe restraints are imposed. Willingness to accept countless alternative true or right world-versions does not mean that everything goes, that tall stories are as good as short ones, that truths are no longer distinguished from falsehoods, but only that truth must be otherwise conceived than as correspondence with a ready-made world. Though we make worlds by making versions, we no more make a world by putting symbols together at random than a carpenter makes a chair by putting pieces of wood together at

random. The multiple worlds I countenance are just the actual worlds made
by and answering to true or right versions.[9]

4. Symbiosis and Relationality

We shall have occasion to return to Goodman's insightful perspective
in chapter five. Before moving on, however, there is one further feature
of the view of reality I am proposing that warrants discussion. In addition
to displaying a dimensional and hierarchical structure, and in addition to
participating in a mediational dynamic whereby these various dimensions disclose and are disclosed by one another, human experienced reality is also ordered symbiotically and relationally. That is, the various
aspects constituting any given dimension of significance exist in a pattern
of mutual interdependence wherein the reality of each is a function of its
relationship to the other. Not only, then, is there a plurality of worlds or
dimensions—none of which exists independently of nor can be reduced
to an account of the others—but within each dimension there is a plurality of aspects or entities that exist in symbiotic, interdependent relationship to each other.

The notion of symbiosis is borrowed from biology. The fundamental
idea is that of two or more life forms living in a balance created by their
mutual dependence such that none can be said to live or maintain itself
apart from the other(s). When developed on a broader scale, this notion
of symbiosis yields the more inclusive concept of an ecological system
wherein each of the participating elements is interdependent upon all the
rest for its livelihood and well-being. Furthermore, the existence and
health of the entire system is a function of the proper balance maintained
by means of this interdependency.

The original Greek meaning of the term *symbiotic* is "life together." It
is in this sense that it is helpful to think of the relationship among the various aspects and entities constituting reality as one of symbiosis. For,
rather than existing independently as separable atoms, they can be seen
best as resulting from mutual interaction, much as a fabric results from
the interweaving of various strands. The constituents of a woven fabric
are termed the warp and the weft; and though they can be distinguished
from each other while the fabric is whole, neither can be said to exist in-

---

[9]Nelson Goodman, *Ways of Worldmaking* (Indianapolis: Hackett Publishing Company,
1978) 2, 3, 94.

dependently apart from the other. To destroy the fabric is to destroy both the warp and the weft, for each gets its reality from the other.

Shifting the image, consider the relationship between two poles in an electromagnetic force-field. We can speak meaningfully of the two poles as different from each other, the one positive and the other negative, but we cannot isolate one from the other or define either without reference to the other. The poles of a magnetic force-field are truly symbiotic: each attains and maintains its reality in and through its relationship to the other. When the force-field is broken up the poles, which are generally said to constitute it, cease to exist. This raises a question to which we shall return shortly, namely which actually constitutes which, the field or the poles? But first, a word about the significance of this notion vis à vis the history of philosophy and the recovery of transcendence.

The idea of the symbiotic character of reality flies in the face of both the classical concept of substance and the modern doctrine of individualism. One of the most persistent and pervasive dogmas in all of Western thought is that of atomism, according to which each entity in the world is essentially distinct from and independent of all others. From Aristotle through Descartes to both Russell and Sartre, the notion of individual substances as the building blocks of reality has dominated the West. Only in recent times has the possibility of conceiving of individuals related to each other by stronger, even determinative ties appeared upon the scene. Pragmatists and phenomenologists, such as George Herbert Mead and Maurice Merleau-Ponty, have made deeply insightful contributions to a symbiotic understanding of the real, especially as it pertains to personal and social existence. Whitehead also has made a powerful case for viewing reality as essentially relational in character. More of this in a moment, however.

The importance of the notion of symbiosis for the recovery of transcendence cannot be overemphasized. For, here again, we are confronted with a quality of experienced reality in which the whole is more than the sum of its parts, in which the more comprehensive dimension is mediated in and through the less. Thus while the symbiotic whole is itself dependent upon its parts, which provide its boundary conditions, the symbiotic whole is more and other than its parts as well. Therefore, the symbiotic unity of the whole transcends yet is not independent of those features of which it is composed. In the case of the electromagnetic force-field, for instance, the positive and negative poles together constitute the force-field, yet they also are transcended by it. Without the poles we do not have a force-field, but when we have the poles we also have a reality that is richer and more comprehensive than two polar entities.

To explore further the notion of symbiosis in relation to that of transcendence, consider the experience of friendship. In any instance of friendship, there exist two or more persons who are related to one another as friends. The persons involved, qua friends, are mutually interdependent. That is to say, neither can relate to the other as a friend by him- or herself, since to be befriended is to exist in a friendship relation. In short, it takes at least two to constitute a friendship. Nevertheless, the reality of the friendship involved is richer and more comprehensive than that of the friends per se. The friendship exists and is experienced as a reality that transcends the individual friends, even though it is conditioned and mediated by them as well.

Friendship clearly is but one of the many relational dimensions of human existence that exhibits this symbiotic, mediational structure. Each of us, along with every other aspect of the world, both human and nonhuman, participates in a myriad of relationships simultaneously. Our existence spreads out in two directions at once—horizontally as we enter into an increasing number of relationships, many of which are symbiotic in nature, and vertically since many (if not most) of these relationships are experienced hierarchically in relation to richness and comprehensiveness. These increased levels of dimensional reality both transcend and are mediated by those out of which they arise. They are disclosed, as I have indicated, in and through the particulars of the mediating dimensions, yet they go beyond them as well.

The preceding brings us to the other aspect of experienced reality that I mentioned at the outset of this section, namely relationality. Perhaps no one has done more to endow the notion of relatedness with special significance than Alfred North Whitehead. His process-oriented approach, whether geared to metaphysics, science, religion, art, or education, is aimed explicitly against viewing reality as being composed of optionally and/or arbitrarily associated individuals. The process view not only stresses the idea that the pattern of developmental change is fundamental to the structure of the world, but it emphasizes the essentially interrelated character of this pattern as well. What Whitehead termed "the fallacy of misplaced concreteness" militates against metaphysical atomism and isolationism as strongly as it does against materialism.

The basic theme and direction of Whitehead's relational understanding of reality is captured in the following quotation:

The notion of 'organism' is combined with that of 'process' in a twofold manner. The community of actual things is an organism; but it is not a static organism. It is an incompletion in process of production. Thus the expansion of the universe in respect to actual things is the first meaning of 'process'; and the universe in any stage of its expansion is the first meaning of 'organism.' In this sense, an organism is a nexus.

Secondly, each actual entity is itself only describable as an organic process. It repeats in microcosm what the universe is in macrocosm. It is a process proceeding from phase to phase, each phase being the real basis from which its successor proceeds towards the completion of the thing in question. Each actual entity bears in its constitution the "reasons" why its conditions are what they are. These "reasons" are the other actual entities objectified for it.[10]

Whitehead's main concern was to counteract the static and passive quality of traditional philosophy by focusing on the central role played by events in the construction of reality. The real is not simply *there;* rather, it *happens*—and this "happening" calls attention to the fact that the "persons, places, and things" of the world arise out of these events and not vice versa. Whitehead contended that "actual occasions" are the fundamental units of reality and that when these units group themselves in space and time, they form a "nexus" or interactive and transitive cluster of being and significance. If these clusters maintain themselves sufficiently, they become objects and persons in the world and are termed "societies" by Whitehead. These actual occasions, nexuses, and societies are claimed to be the properly *concrete* units of reality, as contrasted to the things and persons that derive from them and thus are more abstract.

Put in symbolic form, the relational character of Whitehead's process philosophy can be expressed in this way.[11] Any given reality (X) is constituted as a relationship (R) between (a) and (b) such that with respect to aRb the R is logically prior to the a and b. Traditionally, and perhaps intuitively, we generally think of the relatees (a and b) as more fundamental than the relationship between them (R). Whitehead's contention is that as constituents of the particular relationship in question, a and b are a function of their participation in R; that is, they attain their identity as constituents of R by virtue of being related to each other through it. Thus R must be said to be logically prior to a and b—in much the same way as premises are logically prior, though not necessarily chronologically or experientially prior, to the conclusion that follows from them.

---

[10]Alfred North Whitehead, *Process and Reality* (New York: Free Press, 1929) 214-15.

[11]Here I am employing expressions introduced by Harold Oliver in his book *A Relational Metaphysic* (The Hague: Martinus Nijhoff, 1981) 155ff.

It should be clear that such a relational understanding of experienced reality dovetails nicely with the symbiotic motif presented a bit earlier. In fact, the latter can be thought of as a specific instance of the former. In each, the reality and character of that which is related is a function of the quality and structure of that by virtue of which they are related. Moreover, not only is the reality of the symbiotic constituents of a relationship derived from that relationship, but the latter is properly said to be transcendent of the former while at the same time mediated by them. Such a notion of transcendence is unlike the more traditional, dualistic understanding in that it is grounded in and mediated by the dimensions and particulars that it transcends.

Aristotle contended that although in some sense the form of a given reality is *other* and *more* than the particular material manifestations of it, it nonetheless makes no sense to maintain that it can exist or be known *apart* from them. What I am proposing is the recovery of transcendence by reconceiving of it in immanent terms. God, in this view, can be understood as transcendent in relation to the world without being thought of as existing independently of it. A relational transcendence both offers and requires a more dimensional and mediational concept of the interaction between the divine and the human. Perhaps the relationship between the human mind and the brain is at once the best example of this sort of immanent transcendence and the best model for our understanding God's relation to the world. The mind is transcendent of the brain without being separate from it; it is known in and through the brain—just as our intentions are manifest in and through our behavior, but are not reducible to an account of it.

The symbiotic, relational nature of our particular way of being in the world as both mind and body has been explored by Maurice Merleau-Ponty. He places our embodiment at the axis of our existence, as the most determinative feature of the human form of life. As such, it functions as the base level in the hierarchy of our multidimensional reality. All else is mediated to us in and through it and is known to us only by means of it. Such fundamental aspects of our embodied life as perception, sexuality, and speech are both illuminated and delineated by Merleau-Ponty in terms of their being mediated in and through the body.

More specifically, even our minds and selves are shown to be mediated dimensions of our embodiment. For, they arise and are known only through our mutual interaction concerning our shared goals and through talks within our common environment as embodied persons. By means of our bodies, we learn to participate in common activities and in language, thereby entering into and taking on our humanity. In addition, when we share and enact our ideas and intentions, we do so by means of behavior, both verbal and nonverbal. Finally, when we come to know the world around us, both physical and social, we do so by interacting with things and persons in and through our bodies.

What this establishes is the viability, indeed the necessity, of a notion of transcendence that allows the richer, more comprehensive dimensions of existence to be "beyond" the less rich and comprehensive dimensions while at the same time remaining "within" them. In Merleau-Ponty's penetrating analysis of the pivotal role of the body, we see that precisely this sort of transcendent relationship exists between one's self and one's body. We do not *have* bodies, we *are* bodies; and yet this is not so in a reductionist sense, since in some contexts we distinguish between ourselves and our bodies. Such contexts, however, are not the norm; they are not the basis upon which we come to be ourselves and to know others. Thus they are parasitic on the more paradigmatic cases in which our selves are mediated exclusively in and through our behavior.

Simply because a given intention fails to be embodied, we are not entitled to conclude that intentions, minds, and selves exist independently of our bodies. In fact, just the opposite conclusion would seem to follow, since not only are intentions and selves normally revealed in and through behavior, but even in cases of failure (what J. L. Austin would call a "misfire") we are able to make the distinction between the intention and behavior only on the basis of the fact that in this instance the relationship broke down. Properly speaking, the intention does not exist independently of the behavior; rather, the intended act does not come off as intended. There is no "ghostly essence" left over in such cases, even though there are frustrations, disappointments, and so forth. It is the same with a lie: the proper contrast is not between what one thinks in one's mind and what one says. Rather, there is a conflict between what one says in a given case and what one says and/or does in other cases. In all these situations the mind, the self can be said to transcend any given behavior, but not in the sense of existing apart from it.

This brings us once more to the notion of transcendence in relation to religious reality. Here again my point is that in light of the forgoing considerations, the possibility and advisability of construing divine transcendence as mediated and relational takes on special significance. Conceiving of experienced reality in each and every aspect as structured according to a hierarchy of mediated dimensions opens the way for an understanding of God's relation to the world and human awareness thereof that avoids the pitfalls of traditional dualism without falling victim to one-dimensional reductionism. Just as our minds and selves are mediated in and through our bodies, so God's selfhood can be seen as mediated in and through the various dimensions of the world—from nature and history to politics and art, from science and philosophy to morality and faith.

One analogy that suggests itself is that of the relationship between a small child and its parent. The child's experienced reality is much less rich and inclusive than that of the parent; hence it is appropriate to speak of the latter's world as transcendent of the child's. Nonetheless, they interact in the same world. The parent does not transcend the child's world by being able to leave it or exist independently of it. The two exist in a common world, held together in relationship through their mutual interaction, each being defined to a large degree by the other. Of course, in the explicit sense there are entire dimensions of the parent's existence of which the child knows nothing. Yet these transcendent dimensions impinge upon and are mediated to the child in and through the parent's interaction with the child at his level. The parent's commitments, occupation, worries, decisions, hobbies, and friends all play an implicit yet extremely important role in the child's life.

Moreover, the richness and scope of the parent's life and world can be and are known by the child in and through their mutual interaction. The concerns and celebrations, the struggles and games, the activities and decisions constituting the child's reality all serve as mediating junctures or catalysts of the parent's world. Thus slowly, through repeated and increased participation, the child comes to know and enter into the adult world. It is this notion of transcendence, as dimensional and mediated, that characterizes both the relationship between the parent's world and the child's—the one is at once in and beyond the other—and the relationship between the divine and the human.

Thus, the recovery of transcendence depends upon reconstruing the notion in terms of dimensionality and mediation so as to avoid both dualism and reductionism. Understanding reality as relational and symbiotic is crucial to this reconstruing process, as the forgoing discussion has sought to make clear. In the preface to his monumental work *Phenomenology of Perception*, Merleau-Ponty speaks both of the impossibility of obtaining a direct, unmediated knowledge of the world or "ultimate reality" and of the lack of necessity to do so. Because we are woven into the fabric that constitutes the world, including each other, the only knowledge we can and need to get is available in and through our interaction *within* this fabric. Merleau-Ponty concludes with the following striking image: "Reflection does not withdraw from the world towards the unity of consciousness as the world's basis; it steps back to watch the forms of transcendence fly up like sparks from a fire; it slackens the intentional threads which attach us to the world and thus brings them to our notice."[12]

This image of threads, by means of which we are related to the world and others, focuses the notion of transcendence that I have been urging. For, although the world and others are other than us, and in that sense beyond us, we are yet in a position to know them both by working the threads that connect us and by slackening them. They are as much within and around us as they are beyond us, since we and they are fundamentally two foci of the same reality. It is in this fashion that we can overcome the ontological gap between the mundane and the transcendent built into traditional philosophy all the way from Plato and Descartes to Hume and Kant.

---

[12]Maurice Merleau-Ponty, *Phenomenology of Perception* (New York: Humanities Press, 1962) xiii.

Three

KNOWING:

Knowledge

as Tacit and Interactive

There has been a great deal of discussion about whether ontology or epistemology is primordial in relation to the other. Speculative thinkers generally affirm the former, while analytic thinkers assert the latter. For myself, I think the two are logically simultaneous and symbiotic. That is, both our understanding of and the reality of being and knowing are mutually interdependent. We arrive on the scene, both as infants and as budding thinkers, already involved with both reality and knowledge; they come together as two poles of a unitary experience, and each can only be experienced and understood in relation to the other.

Nevertheless, two chapters of a book cannot be written simultaneously. Thus I began with a chapter on being, on the structure of reality, and shall now move on to a chapter on knowing, on the process of cognition. The main reason for choosing this particular order is that it seems more helpful to explain our interaction with and knowledge of the world after having given an account of its character. Also, of course, the notion of transcendence is usually construed metaphysically rather than epistemologically, so it seemed appropriate to begin with being rather than with knowing.

In the present chapter, then, I shall chart a fresh course toward a recovery of transcendence in relation to the pattern of human awareness and understanding. Affirmations of cognitive encounter with the transcendent can only be appreciated, analyzed, and evaluated after the dynamics of cognition itself have been reflected upon. Broadly speaking, my fundamental claim is that the concept of transcendence has been ruled out by modern epistemology on the basis of an overly narrow understanding of what cognition involves. My guides in the charting of this fresh course will be the works of Michael Polanyi, Maurice Merleau-Ponty, and the mature Ludwig Wittgenstein. These three thinkers, each in his own way, have provided the insights necessary to the construction of a post-modern epistemology and to the possibility of a revitalized notion of transcendence as well.

1. The Explicit and the Tacit

Given that the various aspects of experience are best viewed as dimensional in their relation to one another, what is the nature of the knowing experience for the person situated within these simultaneously interpenetrating dimensions? What are the characteristics of cognitive significance; how is it grasped? The traditional model for understanding cognitive experience has nearly always been some sort of basic distinction between the known and the knower—that is, between what is "given" in experience and the mind to which it is given. Kant brought this approach to prominence, and in recent years the empiricist variation has become increasingly influential.

The major objection to be raised against the traditional approach, which views cognitivity as a function of the relationship between the given (the known) and the dual mind (the knower), pertains to its rigidity. To begin with, a position that attempts to speak of the two entities of the knowing situation as if they were isolated from the other aspects of experience will not jibe with the dimensional analysis set out in the forgoing chapter. Whatever is known participates in a variety of dimensions at the same time. With respect to the knower, any position that seeks to view the knower as functioning with only one avenue of perception at a time is grossly inadequate. Yet this is precisely what "atomistic" and "sense-data" theories of perceptual cognition seek to do when they speak of sounds, colored patches, hardness, and so forth as if each was experienced in isolation from the other. These various aspects of perceptual cognition are, in fact, experienced in concert with each other by the fully integrated senses of the knower.

One other point about the rigidity of the traditional view of cognition bears mentioning. The distinction, and oftentimes dichotomy, that is made between what is given and the one to whom it is given fails to take into account that what is "the given" in one situation for one person may not be "the given" for another person in the same situation. This is true for all levels of experience, from physical perception to moral awareness. The relativity of cognitive significance makes it clear that what is needed is a model for understanding experience that is flexible enough to do justice to the contextual nature of experience without falling into the throes of skepticism.

Rather than thinking of cognitive significance as a static, dualistic relationship between the knower and the known, it is more helpful to think of it as a dynamic, contextual relationship in which the factors and dimensions constituting the knower and the known are subject to a good deal of fluctuation. The contextual boundaries of any situation yielding cognitive awareness are always rough and are determined by a variety of factors. Among these factors are such things as intentionality and purpose, the activity and response of both the knower and the known, and the social and perceptual conventions involved. These contexts exist against the backdrop of a vast number of overlapping continua, such as those that extend between perception and conception, between formal and informal logic, between thought and action, and between objectivity and subjectivity. Thus cognitive significance can arise in any context located anywhere on these various continua, depending upon the way the context is focused by the knowing person.

Two brief examples of the dimensional and contextual nature of cognitive significance should be sufficient. On the perceptual level, consider the experience of being confronted with a picture-puzzle. Here the question of what is "given" is often quite meaningless. On the other hand, it is obvious that one cannot read into the picture-puzzle any configuration whatever. At the same time, the question of what a person "sees" in the picture-puzzle will depend upon a variety of factors, such as what one is told to look for, what one hopes to see, and one's experience with other picture-puzzles. The contextual nature of cognitive significance is dramatically seen when, as the result of an additional clue, a person becomes aware of a pattern that previously had gone unnoticed.

On the moral level, the contextual nature of cognition can be seen in considering a father's relationship to his disobedient son. The father's cognition of the situation, as well as the nature of the son's act, is altered according to the dynamic development of the context. At first the father may perceive the son's disobedience as defiance. Then, in response to the words "I didn't know," he may perceive it as a mistake—or perhaps defiance covered up by a lie. Finally, at the words "I'm sorry, Dad" (uttered in the right tone and circumstances), the father is made aware of the reciprocal nature of the moral realm, for now the focus shifts to him and the possibility of forgiveness. The point is simply that our awareness of cognitive significance, on whatever level, is entirely a function of the factors that form the context.

A thinker who has set a fast pace in the effort to reconstruct contemporary epistemology, and upon whose thought much of the present discussion is based, is Alan Pasch. In summing up his very thorough argument against the traditional view of cognitive significance, he says:

> As the gap between the ordinary and technical kinds of significance becomes wider and empirical significance becomes more of a problem, philosophic attempts to meet the problem become more sophisticated, tend to ignore the ordinary kind of significance, and result in a further widening of the gap. The present account may be understood as seeking to restore the experientially prior kind of significance to philosophic empiricism without losing whatever benefits have been won through concern for a rigid criterion of meaning. The vehicle for restoration is the contextualist theory of significance, which not only prevents the extreme rigidity that leads to suspension of judgment in dealing with empirical contexts but also gives rise to a philosophic concept of significance that does justice to and is continuous with experienced significance. The concept of significance emerging from a contextualist approach is continuous with experienced significance because the latter is contextual, and rigidity is prevented because the contextualist theory is pluralistic, adapting its criteria to whatever context is to be evaluated.[1]

Pasch goes on to outline a theory of cognitivity based upon a distinction between those questions that arise within a context ("internal questions") and those that arise about the context ("external questions"). He argues that those who have sought to push the analysis of meaning down to its ultimate foundation (be it sense-data, atomic facts, objects, etc.) have failed to observe this distinction. Questions of meaning and truth can be answered, but only within a well-defined context. As the focus of attention shifts from the original question to one about the factors making up the original context, the context itself shifts. Thus there is no possibility of ever producing a complete and precise analysis of cognitive meaning

---

[1]Alan Pasch, *Experience and the Analytic* (Chicago: University of Chicago Press, 1958) 202.

in general.[2] Nevertheless, within a given context significance can be discerned, and that is all that is necessary.

> Precision, like cognitive significance, tends to be pursued for its own sake. This absence of ulterior motive is harmless when precision carries clearness in its wake and when whatever has cognitive significance has empirical significance also. But the fact is that it is not maximum precision which governs our cognitive behavior but significant precision. The limit to the degree of precision we attain in low-level cognition is determined by significance in the sense in which it is experienced, which is to say, by empirical significance. We strive, in any cognitive situation, for the maximum degree of precision that is relevant or important or valuable in that situation.[3]

Michael Polanyi has made what might well be the most lasting contribution to the construction of a postmodern epistemology. Like Pasch, he has had the insight to draw several crucial distinctions (not dichotomies!) that provide guidelines for any attempt to overcome the epistemology dualism of our day. Although I willingly credit Professor Polanyi with providing the direction of my thought, I do not want to saddle him with the responsibility for the extrapolations I make from his thought.

The first of Polanyi's important distinctions upon which I wish to build is the one between "focal" and "subsidiary" awareness.[4] In any given cognitive context, there are some factors of which knowing subjects are aware because they are directing their attention to them ("focal awareness"). In the same context there are also factors of which the knower is aware even when not focusing on them ("subsidiary awareness"). By way of example, in the context of reading these words the reader focuses attention on their meaning, not on the letters of which they are composed nor even upon the words themselves. Nonetheless, it is obvious that the reader is subsidiarily aware of both the letters and the words.

Clearly this distinction, like all contextual distinctions, is a relative one. In other words, one can direct attention to those factors of which formerly one had only subsidiary awareness, thereby becoming focally aware of them. In like manner, one can become subsidiarily aware of those fac-

---

[2]Ibid., 212-40.

[3]Ibid., 209-10.

[4]See esp. chs. 4 and 5 of Michael Polanyi, *Personal Knowledge* (New York: Harper & Row, 1964); also ch. 1 of *The Tacit Dimension* (Garden City NY: Doubleday, 1966).

tors of which formerly one was focally aware. This is obvious with respect to the above example of letter, words, and meaning. It also is true about other levels of experience, such as the psychological, the moral, and possibly the religious. In all these cases the cognitive context is brought into being by the knowing subject's "attending from" that of which one is focally aware. Polanyi summarizes it this way:

> When we are relying on our awareness of something (A) for attending to something else (B), we are but subsidiarily aware of A. The thing B to which we are thus focally attending, is then the meaning of A. The focal object B is always identifiable, while things like A, of which we are subsidiarily aware, may be unidentifiable. The two kinds of awareness are mutually exclusive: when we switch our attention to something of which we have hitherto been subsidiarily aware, it loses its previous meaning. Such is briefly, *the structure of tacit knowing.*[5]

The major epistemological point to be drawn from this distinction is that not only is cognitive awareness exclusively a function of contextual significance, it is a function of a continuum between focal and subsidiary awareness as well. Knowledge as awareness simply cannot be limited to that of which we are focally aware. In order for there even to be a context in which one can be focally aware of some factors, there must also be some factors of which one is only subsidiarily aware. In short, one must have a "place to stand"—to attend *from*—in order to be able to attend to anything at all. This contextual interpretation of cognitive awareness avoids the pitfalls of both skepticism and those positions (be they rationalistic or empiricistic) that demand indubitability. Contrary to the former, knowledge remains a realizable possibility, while contrary to the latter it does so only within flexible contexts.

A second distinction made by Polanyi is between the two poles of what might be called "the activity continuum." All human activity can be placed on a scale somewhere between "conceptualization"—which is most often verbal— and "embodiment"—which pertains to nonverbal behavior. The vast majority of human behavior is an inextricable mixture of both verbal and bodily activity. Even simple thinking (to say nothing of talking) is likely to be accompanied by certain bodily movements; alternatively, bodily action is likely to have corresponding mental (and even verbal) ac-

---

[5]Polanyi, *Personal Knowledge*, x.

tivity. Athletes talk to themselves or to their opponents; sailors and workcrews sing as they work; and lovers feel it necessary to "whisper sweet nothings" to each other.

There is a sense in which every activity on this continuum can be said to involve making a judgment. In addition to assertions and thought processes, which obviously involve judgments, it can be shown that even such so-called noncognitive verbalizations as "hello" and "oh!" imply a judgment about the situation in which they are spoken. This is why we say that a ballplayer "misjudged" the ball or that a motorist "misjudged" the speed of the other car. Any given human act is performed within a context that renders it an act of judgment in relation to that context.

An important corollary to this activity continuum is the fact that any human behavior, to the extent that it implies making a judgment, involves a knowledge claim and can be evaluated as either appropriate (true) or inappropriate (false). Thus there is no room for a hard-and-fast distinction between "saying" as a cognitive activity and "doing" as a noncognitive activity. Whether a particular act is verbal or nonverbal is always a question of degree, but there is no question of whether or not an act implies a cognitive judgment. To some extent all acts do.

The other side of this corollary is that all knowledge claims involve the commitment, or "personal backing," of the one making the claim. The point, in short, is simply that even though a knowledge claim is implicit in a given action, be it verbal or nonverbal, the person involved is nonetheless responsible for substantiating this claim. We hold people accountable for their reflex actions as well as for their verbal promises. All human activity is predicated upon the reality of responsible commitment.

The first distinction in this section was between focal and subsidiary awareness and the second was between conceptual and bodily activity. When these two sets of distinctions are related to one another, the result is a third distinction between explicit and tacit knowledge. The relationship can be visualized by diagraming the awareness continuum and the activity continuum as dimensions that intersect each other. When the poles of subsidiary awareness and bodily activity are related, the result is tacit knowledge. As every awareness and activity is a mixture of its respective poles, so every form of knowledge is a mixture of both explicit and tacit elements. In other words, relating the first two continua in this way produces yet a third continuum—the cognitivity continuum—between the explicit and tacit poles.

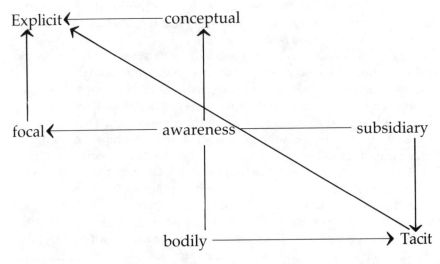

To put this distinction another way, every context in which cognitive significance is present contains both tacit and explicit factors. That is, the context exists somewhere on the continuum between these two poles. The interaction between those factors of which the subject is focally aware and the conceptual response gives rise to explicit knowledge. Such is the case when a person attends to and names an object in the perceptual field. The interaction between those factors of which the subject is subsidiarily aware and the more nonverbal, bodily response gives rise to tacit knowledge. Such is the case when the person attending to and naming an object in the perceptual field is not conscious of, but still must be said to know, the functioning of the senses and discriminatory powers that render explicit knowledge possible. That a person knows these tacit factors can be made clear by asking him or her to focus on them, whereupon the person may become quite articulate about the movement of head and hands, and about the rational steps necessary in identifying an object. But then some other factors will be supplying the tacit context within which this new focusing is taking place.

Explicit knowledge, then, is the sort of knowledge with which we are quite familiar. In fact, for all practical purposes, it is the only form of knowledge that nearly all philosophers of the Western tradition, whether rationalist or empiricist, have been willing to admit. Indeed, it is this refusal to think of knowledge as a continuum that has led to the dichotomy between cognitive and noncognitive judgments. Polanyi's continuum approach to the nature of cognitive significance is very closely related to Pasch's contextual approach. When these concepts are combined, the groundwork has been laid for the construction of a more adequate epistemology. A contextual and continuum interpretation of cognitivity allows for making relative distinctions, but avoids the necessity of establishing dichotomies between judgments of fact and judgments of value.

There are two further points about the relation between explicit and tacit knowledge that need to be discussed by way of coming to a firmer understanding of the latter. Both of these points are made in the following paragraph from Polanyi:

> Things of which we are focally aware can be explicitely [sic] identified; but no knowledge can be made *wholly explicit*. For one thing, the meaning of language, when in use, lies in its tacit component; for another, to use language involves actions of our body of which we have only a subsidiary awareness. Hence, tacit knowing is more fundamental than explicit knowing: *we can know more than we can tell and we can tell nothing without relying on our awareness of things we may not be able to tell.*[6]

Polanyi's main thesis is that tacit knowledge is not only a legitimate form of knowledge, but that it is *logically prior* to explicit knowledge. In any situation the subject tacitly relies upon a large variety of factors in order to know any factors explicitly. Moreover, although what is known tacitly in one context may well be known explicitly in another context, Polanyi insists that some tacit knowledge can never be known explicitly. In short, as not all words can be defined, so not all knowledge can be explicated.

What sort of things can be said to be examples of tacit knowledge? Polanyi often discusses bodily and perceptual skills as exemplifying tacit knowledge. All of us walk, swim, shoot basketballs, and the like without being able to articulate this knowledge in words. In addition, we all are able to recognize another person's face in a crowd of thousands without being able to say how we do it. A more complex and more important example of tacit knowledge is the ability to grasp the concept of "meaning." Child and philosopher alike are unable to be explicit about the meaning of the term *meaning*, but it is obvious that they both know what it means. The best way of accounting for the logical primitiveness of meaning is in

---

[6]Ibid.

terms of tacit knowledge. The problem with the seeming circularity of the concept of meaning is similar to that which traditionally has arisen over the concept of knowledge. This latter difficulty received its classic statement in Plato's *Meno*, and as stated there provides strong substantiation for Polanyi's position on the necessity of tacit knowledge: "The *Meno* shows conclusively that if all knowledge is explicit, i.e., capable of being clearly stated, then we cannot know a problem or look for its solution. And the *Meno* also shows, therefore, that if problems nevertheless exist, and discoveries can be made by solving them, we can know things, and important things, that we cannot tell."[7]

One aspect of tacit knowledge that bears special mention is that which pertains to the role of the body. As noted, it is necessary to view bodily activity as a form of cognitive judgment. Another way of putting this is to maintain that our bodies function as instruments to attain knowledge that is often tacit. Thus tacit knowledge is of necessity more closely related to bodily awareness and activity. Motor knowledge, for instance, can be obtained only by means of what Polanyi calls "indwelling." The only way to know some things is to indwell or participate in them. Now, since all knowledge is to some extent tacit, it becomes apparent that indwelling is an important aspect of every cognitive situation. There is always a sense in which the process of coming to know anything, be it an object or a person, is dependent upon empathetic indwelling. As Polanyi puts it:

> We know another person's mind by the same integrative process by which we know life. A novice trying to understand the skill of a master, will seek *mentally* to combine his movements to the pattern to which the master combines them *practically*. By such exploratory indwelling the novice gets the feel of the master's skill. Chess players enter into a master's thought by repeating the games he played. *We experience a man's mind as the joint meaning of his actions* by dwelling in his actions from outside.[8]

Perhaps a summary will prove helpful at this point. Knowledge is to be viewed as a continuum between the tacit and explicit poles. All cognitive situations involve a blending of these two polar factors. Explicit knowledge is defined as a function of focal awareness and conceptual (or

---

[7]Polanyi, *Tacit Dimension*, 22.

[8]Michael Polanyi, "The Logic of Tacit Inference," *Philosophy* 41 (January 1966): 14.

verbal) activity. As such, it exhibits such characteristics as precise analysis, verbal articulation, descriptive identification, observational objectivity, and an absolute distinction between the knower and the known (subject and object). Tacit knowledge, on the other hand, is defined as a function of subsidiary awareness and bodily activity. As such, it exhibits such characteristics as intuitive discovery, bodily expression, holistic recognition, embodied subjectivity, and a contextual distinction between the knower and the known.

2. Embodiment and Interaction

The role of the body in Polanyi's epistemological thought serves as an excellent bridge to this present section. Perhaps counter-intuitively, the general shape of my design for a recovery of transcendence from an epistemological perspective centers around the role of the body, not the mind (or spirit or soul). To my way of thinking, the Western proclivity for stressing the privileged position of the mind in relation to knowledge has led to the difficulties associated with traditional dualism. A postmodern epistemology must avoid the intellectualistic hegemony that has given rise to the present stalemate between "the ghost in the machine" on the one hand and the "ghostless machine" of behaviorism on the other hand.

In his pivotal and deservedly well-known book *The Idea of a Social Science and Its Relation to Philosophy*,[9] Peter Winch sets forth a case against the possibility of obtaining objectivity in the social sciences. Indeed, it has been suggested that a more accurate title for Winch's book would be The Very Idea of a Social Science! From a Wittgensteinian perspective, Winch established a dichotomy between the natural sciences and the social sciences, affirming objectivity in the former while denying it in the latter.

The basis of Winch's dichotomy is not the traditional existentialist contention that while we can know the physical world indirectly from the "outside," we know ourselves directly and most truly from the "inside." Rather, he argues that the concepts, laws, and rules of inference by means of which we explain physical reality are not part of that reality; thus they can be applied to it objectively and can be said to yield scientific understanding. On the other hand, the conceptual schema by means of which we seek to explain social reality is, in fact, a vital part of that very reality

---

[9]Peter Winch, *The Idea of a Social Science and Its Relation to Philosophy* (London: Routledge and Kegan Paul, 1958).

and can only be applied by one who is a participant in that reality. The notion of scientific objectivity in social understanding is therefore out of the question.

What distinguishes Winch's approach from the standard romanticist and/or existentialist approach is that rather than maintaining the primacy of internal, subjective, and private personal knowledge over against cold, objective, and public scientific knowledge, Winch affirms the primacy of the sociolinguistic conceptual schema that serves as the matrix for all knowledge. Thus social reality is seen as linguistically constituted and not subject to objective scientific understanding. Following Wittgenstein, Winch concludes that the human form of life, or social reality, can only be understood from within, since understanding itself is a social phenomenon.

While I agree with Winch concerning the basis and texture of conceptual understanding vis-à-vis social reality, I urge that we make similar moves with respect to physical reality. In other words, I am not prepared to grant natural science the sort of "objectivity," or immunity in relation to the structure of human understanding, with which Winch endows it. In short, natural science does not enjoy the sort of objectivity traditionally ascribed to it (and too readily by Winch!), since all human understanding is predicated on embodiment. We interact with the physical and social dimensions of our world through our bodies and through speech, and any understanding of either of these dimensions must take this dual interaction into account.

What Winch overlooks is the possibility that, in parallel fashion, the fundamental characteristic of human existence that renders knowledge of physical reality possible is our participation in that dimension of our world by means of our bodies. Like nearly every Western thinker before him, at least until very recent times, Winch approaches the whole question of cognitivity as an intellectualist. However, not only are we part and parcel of the physical world in much the same way as we are enmeshed in social reality, it is also true that our conceptual activity exists symbiotically with our physical behavior patterns and cannot be understood apart from them.

Winch's mentor, Wittgenstein, clearly grasped this in his notion of "language-games" as forms of human social activity. Sad to say, most commentators on Wittgenstein's later work fail to do much, if anything, with the behavioral side of his work. He continually stresses the symbiotic quality of cognitivity, involving both thought *and* action—as the following quotation makes amply clear:

"So you are saying that human agreement decides what is true and what is false?"—It is what human beings *say* that is true and false; and they agree in the *language* they use. That is not agreement in opinions but in form of life.

If language is to be a means of communication there must be agreement not only in the definitions but also (queer as this may sound) in judgments. This seems to abolish logic, but does not do so.—It is one thing to describe methods of measurement, and another to obtain and state results of measurements. But what we call "measuring" is partly determined by a certain constancy in results of measurement.[10]

Our understanding of any aspect or dimension of experienced reality can only arise from and be based in our participation in that very feature of the world itself. We know social reality only as we so function as members of a community, and especially as we function through the use of language. In like manner, we know physical reality only as we operate in relationship to it through our bodies, both in speech and action.

It was the ubiquitous character of language and its role in cognitive activity that for so many centuries caused philosophers to ignore it in their deliberations. It is certainly to the credit of twentieth-century analytic thinkers, especially Russell and Wittgenstein, that this deficiency has been to some degree overcome. Many thinkers, both within the Anglo and Continental traditions, have contributed to our increased awareness of the importance of language in cognitive activity. The list includes G. E. Moore, J. L. Austin, John Wisdom, Martin Heidegger, H. G. Gadamer, Paul Ricoeur, and many others.

I suspect that this same ubiquitous character of our embodiment has caused philosophers to overlook its centrality in the cognitive process. Certainly the rationalist tradition is well known for its almost total avoidance, if not debasement, of the role of the body in human understanding. To be sure, empiricists have continually talked of the experiential basis of all knowledge, but when one gets down to cases it becomes evident that even here the primary, if not exclusive, interest lies in the mind's reception of perceptions, in the ideas resulting from sensation. One searches in vain for anything like a systematic consideration of tactile interaction, movement in space, and the role of bodily skill in the acquisition of knowledge in the works of Locke, Hume, Russell, Ayer, and Chisholm. Even Kant, for all of his talk of having effected a "Copernican revolu-

---

[10]Ludwig Wittgenstein, *Philosophical Investigations* (New York: Macmillan, 1953) 241-42.

tion," continued to deal with the "objects of thought" *after* they were fil-
tered through the categories of understanding.

Only in recent phenomenology, particularly in the work of Maurice
Merleau-Ponty, do we find thinkers who acknowledge that our way of
being-in-the-world is structured by our embodiment—there is no knowledge apart from that which is mediated through our physicality, movement, and interaction with our bodies (both animate and inanimate) in
space. Very little has been done on the implications of this embodiment
for the activity known as scientific investigation. Polanyi's work, that of
a practicing scientist, is an important exception.

We are "geared" into the world by means of two main media or modes,
language and our bodies. We can only know reality— indeed, reality only
comes into existence and takes shape for us—as we interact in our physical and social environments through our bodies and through speech.
Thus it makes no sense to speak of reality in and of itself (Kant's *Ding an
sich*), not because it is beyond the reach of our minds, but rather because
it is nothing with which we have to do. In Wittgenstein's phrasing, such
talk has no place in our lives, except as it serves to remind us that experienced reality is always capable of changing and thereby changing our
ideas of it.

We are not left, however, in the position of the skeptic or the complete
relativist. Neither are we closed off from the world, trapped in the famous "egocentric predicament." Rather, we continue to engage and be engaged by and with the world in and through our bodies and our speech.
Its reality and nature are mediated to us as we interact with it, responding to and altering it. Although we cannot get outside our relationship to
the world in order to observe either ourselves or the world individually,
we can, do, and must continue to engage the world—in both its physical
and social dimensions—thereby coming to understand it, ourselves, and
the nature of cognitivity in the process. To borrow Merleau-Ponty's image, we can "slacken the threads" by which we are connected to the world
and thereby come to know the nature of those threads without letting go
of them on the one hand (skepticism) or assuming they are incorrigible
on the other hand (foundationalism).

One of the fundamental difficulties in the Western epistemological
tradition is the almost exclusive reliance on visual perception as the paradigmatic cognitive experience. From Plato and Aristotle down through
Locke, Kant, and Russell, vision has been used as the root metaphor and
primary example of what it means to know. While vision is obviously extremely important in human experience (though blind people certainly

have cognitive process), it must be remembered that it is but one of the physical senses whereby we encounter the world. One cannot but wonder what the history of philosophy might read like had some other sense, say touch (as with certain African and Eskimo cultures) or hearing (as to some extent with the ancient Hebrews), become the paradigm of knowing.

First, it must be stressed that vision is essentially a passive mode of perception. Objects and qualities pass before our eyes, in and out of our field of vision, with little or no effort on our part. (Incidentally, there is some evidence that children born without arms and legs, and thus unable to move in space, never develop depth perception.) It is this passive quality of visual sensation that gives rise to thinking of scientific investigation, and the knowledge derived from it, as based on observation. In fact, science is based more fundamentally on interaction with nature than on mere observation. Even observation can be done only after one has placed oneself in the proper relation to, and selected the appropriate features of, the phenomenon in question. Indeed, the very heart of the scientific method is the crucial experiment, which involves the manipulation and control of nature, and the experiment itself must be designed and/or constructed.

Even more significant, however, is the fact that none of the above activities could be carried out unless the scientist(s) involved had acquired the necessary skills (both in learning and understanding) that go along with the employment of the crucial concepts and inferences involved. These skills, in turn, are not acquired in the abstract but in practice under the supervision of an expert—they must be *done*, not simply thought about. Thus there can be no scientific knowledge apart from "somatic knowledge."

Because of our particular intellectual heritage, we are prone to say "Well, of course these bodily aspects are necessary to the scientific enterprise, but they are not what makes something count as knowledge." Similarly, we often encounter the remark, "Well, to be sure, scientific ideas emerge out of the creative activity of the mind, but such things are a matter of psychology, not epistemology." I submit that these polite nods to the nonintellectualistic aspects of our cognitive experience simply will not do. An account of what constitutes human knowledge that leaves out the role of the body will be both incomplete and misleading: not only will it be one-sided and thus inaccurate, but it will dictate the character of epistemological investigation as well. In a word, such intellectualism will function, indeed has functioned, as a self-fulfilling prophecy.

Second, it remains true that because of our traditional reliance on vision as the paradigm of cognitive experience, we have come to think of ourselves (our minds) as separated from reality (à la Kant) in the same way we are differentiated from the objects that we view. Epistemic distance, and thus truth and error, has been patterned after spatial distance in sight. Other senses, especially touch, do not lead to such a radical dichotomy between the knower and the known; they point instead to a more symbiotic, interactionist epistemological posture. We do not observe the world passively and at a distance. Instead, we are engaged with and by it through speech and perception, both of which are grounded in embodiment. Our body is our entry point into the world, the medium through and in which our reality is constituted. To change the metaphor, our body is the *axis* around which the world and reality revolve in continuous dynamic relationship.

It is only because we are embodied that we can understand physical reality. (Winch makes the same point differently by saying it is our participation in social reality that enables us to understand it.) Solidity, motion, growth, and force are comprehendible as concepts because we participate in them in and through our bodies. We do not simply observe such qualities in the world—we embody them, they define our place in the world. More pointedly, we understand the notion of *causation* not because we observe a billiard ball collide with another (à la Hume), not because our minds are structured according to such an intellectual category (à la Kant), but because we exist as active, causal *agents*. We encounter causal factors at work within and upon us; we "body-forth" our intentions and decisions in the world, causing things to happen. If we did not occupy and move in space, and in relation to other bodies, we would be unable to understand such notions as are usually ascribed to nature. In short, we would have no scientific knowledge.

Third, it is extremely important to bear in mind that our embodied experience is *synaesthetic* in character. We encounter reality as holistic, integrated beings who interact with the world in and through all the dimensions of bodily existence simultaneously. Too frequently, those who have sought to understand perception have made the mistake of isolating one mode of sensation from the others, the better to focus it. Once again the "atomistic fallacy" has been operative ("divide and conquer"), a fallacy that Gestalt research has long since exposed and, one hopes, put to rest. We do *not* experience and know the world by constructing it out of various and diverse sense-data that happen to come packaged together fairly consistently (as with phenomenalism). Rather, the world is experienced by us as we interact with its different features holistically. We see, feel, hear, and smell within contexts and events that arise as meaningful wholes through our intentional, responsive activity. How and what we see is much affected by what and how we are hearing, touching, and smelling at the same time— and vice versa. Interesting research has been done along this line in connection with the notion of key in music. Trained keyboard and string musicians can recognize what key a particular performance was originally played in after the music has been put through a computer that changes nothing but the key. These musicians may comment "Well, I'm hearing it in E, but it was played in F"—and it is not incidental that all the while they move and "listen" to their fingers, as if they themselves were doing the playing.

What is frequently overlooked, however, is the tacit character of the cognitive processes that underlie the explicit processes sketched out above. Not only is the physical reality we experience and know equally enmeshed in the linguistic and conceptual dimension of our existence, but more important for our present purposes, our knowledge of nature is equally embedded in our own sharing of the physicality of nature. Our embodiment provides the tacit matrix out of which our ability to understand physical reality arises. When this tacit matrix is acknowledged, and any sound epistemology must acknowledge it, the limitations of the traditional concept of objectivity stand revealed.

But such knowledge does not come about through simple exposure alone. It is the interaction between subsidiary awareness and bodily activity that yields tacit knowledge. We come into the world on the move: sucking, grasping, wiggling, and making noises. We do not simply "receive" data (whether on a blank tablet, as with Locke and Hume, or through an intellectual filter system, as with Kant); rather, we engage, alter, and are altered by objects, persons, and events constituting our world. We encounter the various features of reality as meaningful wholes and we are drawn into their vortex, or perhaps we inject ourselves into their orbit, as the case may be. It is this interaction, at the subsidiary level, that produces tacit knowledge.

The radical significance of tacit knowing can only be appreciated when it is seen as the ground out of which all explicit knowing grows. Tacit knowing is necessarily logically prior to explicit knowing (in the sense that premises are logically prior though not necessarily experientially prior to conclusion), since (1) in no particular context *can* we explicate every aspect of the cognitive dimension involved (as Polanyi says, "We always know more than we say") and (2) in no particular context *need* we explicate all that our knowledge rests upon in order to justify a knowledge claim. Informal justification always underlies formal justification, as Aristotle (deduction ends in induction and induction ends in recognition), Gödel (no conceptual system can be shown to be both internally consistent and self-contained), and Wittgenstein (explanations come to an end, otherwise they would not be explanations) have all established.

The specific characteristic of tacit knowing that is especially relevant here is its special relationship to embodiment. Tacit knowledge is acquired through physically *indwelling* that which is to be known. This is most obvious in the acquisition of skills, while it is less obvious but no less significant at more sophisticated levels, such as those of personal, social, and moral awareness. In the words of John Dewey, at the primordial level we learn by doing. By putting ourselves physically into walking, speaking, swimming, dancing, and so forth—and *only* by so doing—we learn these actions. In like fashion, by bodily interacting with persons, ideas, and institutions we come to know them. These latter things cannot really be understood by means of explicit instruction and contemplation, as Winch has clearly shown.

At this juncture it is common to fall back on the standard dichotomy between "knowing *that*" and "knowing *how*," granting cognitivity to the former and denying it to the latter. But this dichotomy is simply a reification of the traditional dogma that is herein challenged. It is all very nice to limit knowledge to that which can be explicated and substantiated by means of propositions, but it hardly fits the way knowledge is experienced in life, whether at the ordinary or scientific level. To begin with, the line between the two "kinds" of knowledge is not easily drawn, as Wittgenstein's remarks about the symbiotic character of the concept of measurement and the activity of measuring make clear. Second, the fact remains that all propositional knowledge arises out of, must be understood in terms of, and can only be justified by means of nonpropositional knowledge that has been incorporated into the perceptual, kinesthetic, and conceptual skills of the knower.

In an extremely interesting and significant book, *What Computers Can't Do*, Hubert Dreyfus has set forth a convincing case for the view that computers cannot, in principle, *think* as humans do, not because they do not have human minds, but because they do not have human *bodies*. His point is similar to Winch's, in that he argues that it is by participating in social reality that knowledge thereof arises, but Dreyfus differs from Winch in that he contends that we can only participate through our embodiment. The subtleties of the human form of life cannot be taught by explicit rule and instruction, but must be caught by indwelling the procedures in question. Only against the backdrop of embodied experience will propositional knowledge become comprehensible and useful.

Tacit knowledge is incorporated into our bodies, and though "it cannot be said, it shows itself" in the warp and weft of the cognitive fabric within which the pattern of explicit knowledge comes into focus. Scientific activity and knowledge can only exist as the result of the skills acquired by practicing scientists who form a common community. Thus we can only come to understand the physical world through participating in it bodily, thereby acquiring the skills to grasp it—both in the literal sense and in the sense of conceptualizing about it.

A slightly different way to formulate my main concern in this section is in terms of Heisenburg's "principle of indeterminacy." In the field of subatomic physics it has been established that it is impossible to determine *both* the velocity *and* the position of a quantum of energy because any attempt to do so must, logically, introduce energy (light rays) into that which is being observed, thereby affecting it. If this is true for physics, how much more true must it be for such fields as psychology, politics, and art, to say nothing about religion. There simply is no such thing as "uninvolved" knowledge. Knowing is a relational reality, a process that entails both the knower and the known interacting with each other in a common context.

This does not, contrary to popular opinion, render all judgments subjective and equally unreliable. Rather, it reminds us that even our processes designed to eliminate significant bias, which are generally effective, are themselves processes that we have developed and agreed upon as a result of our common tasks and interactions. Thus, not only is our knowledge of reality, both physical and social, a function of our engagement with it, but our criteria for evaluating knowledge claims are also a function of our shared, embodied form of life, our common, human way of being in the world.

3. The Personal and the Social

Throughout the first half of the present century, existentialists have made us aware of the so-called subjective side of all attempts to know the truth. Not only are we limited by our individual and cultural biases, but each and every knowledge claim entails a degree of personal involvement that carries us beyond the boundaries set by reason and evidence. Moreover, we are reminded by such thinkers that with respect to the matters of utmost importance in human life—matters of values, meaning, and faith—the results of objective logic and science are essentially useless. Such considerations can and should be based in individual commitment alone.

While there is a great deal of value in what the existentialists urge, it is important to move very carefully when surrounded by such long-standing and significant issues. Some have employed this mode of thought in the service of positive irrationalism, which undercuts itself by proving too much; for, if *every* commitment is justified, *none* is justified. Others have concluded from this that since no real knowledge is possible, skepticism and absolute relativism are unavoidable. This conclusion not only flies in the face of the broad scope of human experience; it also undercuts the very possibility of coming to conclusions at all.

In general, it is self-defeating to attempt to counterbalance the tyranny of objectivism by extolling the virtues of subjectivism. What needs to be done, first of all, is to establish the viability of a bipolar (the tacit and the explicit) understanding of the cognitivity dimension of human experience, together with the embodied and interactive character of knowledge acquisition. This was the major concern of the two previous sections. The burden of this and the next section is to explore and chart the contours of epistemic responsibility in terms of the roles played by personal commitment, social processes, and justificatory criteria.

In the modern intellectual climate, complete objectivity has generally been taken as both possible and necessary to the attainment of knowledge. In recent decades it has been increasingly, if begrudgingly admitted, that it is impossible to achieve complete objectivity, that all cognitivity is, unfortunately, "contaminated" by certain subjective factors.

This concession, however, has not resolved the tension between what William James called the tough- and the tender-minded among us. The former still seek to minimize the subjective element, while the latter continue to maximize it. What is needed is an altogether fresh way of thinking about the relationship between the knower and the known.

The traditional dichotomy between the objective and the subjective in modern philosophical and theological thought has had disastrous results with respect to the possibility of transcendence. Those who extol the virtues of objectivity—be they rationalists or empiricists—contend that if the notion of transcendence cannot be explicated in terms of the criteria of logic and/or scientific fact, it is not a meaningful concept. It is, of course, generally implied or conceded that transcendence cannot be so explicated. On the other hand, those who sing the praises of subjectivity—be they existentialists or deconstructionists—either relegate transcendence to the realm of the personal or dismiss it as irrelevant at best and illusory at worst.

The first step necessary to overcome this epistemological dichotomy is one that enables us to *affirm* rather than *concede* the role of the personal in human cognitivity without simultaneously ignoring the legitimate concern for public criteria and epistemic responsibility. If our account of the goal and process of knowing results in forcing us to apologize, as a matter of principle, for failing to attain it, there must be something wrong with our account. Instead of defining knowledge in terms of that which cannot be obtained, we ought rather to define it in terms of what actually takes place when human beings are said to achieve knowledge.

The first move here is to acknowledge that knowing is an activity rather than a state. Knowing is something that people *do* rather than something they *have*; it is an achievement rather than a condition. When we say of people that they "have knowledge" concerning a certain topic, what we mean is that in specific circumstances (such as a test or a concrete task), they are able to perform or accomplish what is required. In this sense it is admissible to speak of knowledge being personal or subjective.

To be sure, it is important to guard against trickery, rote memory, lucky guesses, and the like. However, it is not necessary to postulate a private state of mind that "contains" knowledge in order to cover this flank. We often do, of course, know more than we say, or think of things that we find no occasion to use, but such cases are parasitic on cases in which we do put our knowledge to use. We do not first store things in our minds and then use them; rather, first we do make use of things, and only later do we build up a reservoir of knowledge. Moreover, the test of whether or not we know something is fundamentally whether or not we can put it to use in some way.

The next move is to acknowledge that all knowledge is *someone's* knowledge. Knowing is, after all, something that persons do, and thus it is appropriate to call it personal in nature. Owing to the pressures of the "cult of objectivity," there has been a strong tendency to think and talk as if knowledge can exist without a knowing subject. It is not necessary to become a subjectivist in order to admit that knowing—like cooking, loving, and learning—is something that people do; there is no need to pretend that this is not so nor to be embarrassed by it. Moreover, any account of human knowledge that ignores this personal element will not only be incomplete, it will be misleading as well.

Frequently, we are told that while these personal factors are relevant to the *psychology* of knowledge, they are not relevant to epistemology. But this makes sense only if one first assumes that questions of criteria can be separated from questions of process—and it is precisely this assumption that I am now challenging. My claim is that to separate the consideration of criteria from that of process is to distort one's understanding of what it means to know. After all, criteria are developed by persons in the give-and-take of the actual process of coming to know in concrete situations; they arise out of and must in the final analysis answer to human cognitive activity. Our criteria must be decisively altered if they do not function well in relation to our common tasks and purposes. This is exactly the case we are now facing with respect to the relation between objectivity and subjectivity in contemporary epistemology. The criteria of objectivism are too narrow to fit the actual practices and procedures constituting the knowing process.

A third move in the task of restructuring epistemology, so as to incorporate the personal dimension, is to accredit our own knowledge-seeking and -achieving capacities. Rather than trying to base our claims to knowledge in processes and objects external to the knowing subject, we ought to acknowledge straightforwardly that knowledge is a function of our own embodied interaction with our environment. In addition, whenever a person lays claim to knowledge or even denies knowledge in a particular situation, he or she takes a personal stand. In effect, each and every knowledge claim entails a commitment to and confidence in our own ability to perceive, discern, and judge the nature of that with which we have to do, to distinguish between truth and error. Without this element of personal epistemic responsibility, the notion of knowledge makes no sense whatever.

Whenever truth is known, then, someone or some group of persons must affirm it and be prepared to stand behind this affirmation. Truths and knowledge do not float freely in some rarefied, objective vacuum; rather, they are achieved in the push-and-pull of human activity and must receive "personal backing" in order to be considered as cognitively significant. There is nothing subjective about all this, any more than all speech acts and affirmations—including the one that claims that every knowledge claim is subjective—can be said to be subjective. All cognitive affirmations are affirmed and evaluated by individual knowers who trust their own ability to discern and appraise what is going on around them. This is true of everyone—from the tiny child selecting a ball from his toy box to the theoretic scientist postulating the structure of subatomic reality. There is no knowledge apart from a knower.

Because of our fascination with "propositional knowledge," we have allowed ourselves to be deceived into thinking that knowledge can exist without a knower. We speak of the truth or falsehood of this or that proposition, of the importance of distinguishing between "knowledge *of* " and "knowledge *that*," and of the qualitative difference between analytic and synthetic propositions, all as if these were not "judgment calls" that in the final analysis have to be affirmed or denied by individual human knowers. The concern with overcoming subjective bias has misled us into speaking of knowledge in antiseptic terminology, a practice that tends to obscure the personal basis and character of all human cognitivity.

The point here is *not* that somehow our personal involvement in the knowing process renders our cognitive claims veridical (à la existentialism) or impossible (à la skepticism). Rather, the point is that it is we who make and judge between cognitive claims, and any epistemology that ignores this will be both incomplete and misleading. There can be no knowledge apart from the confidence and affirmations of knowing subjects, and the criteria employed in this process arise from and must answer to these realities, not vice versa. Both objectivism and subjectivism must be set aside in favor of an approach that acknowledges both that knowledge is *real* and that it is personal; far from being in opposition, these two qualities constitute the matrix that provides both the necessary and the sufficient conditions for any knowledge whatsoever.

All assertions aim at being understood as well as at being true; these are the conditions that render speech and cognitivity both possible and actual. Our personal involvement or "backing," far from undercutting truth and knowledge, provides the "universal intent" that undergirds the significance and viability of human cognition. Our intending or aiming at what is true universally not only eliminates the threat of skepticism, but it establishes the integral character of the personal dimension in cognitive activity. After all, it is persons who intend and aim, even as it is persons who know and fall into error. If I or you say "The cat is on the mat," it is I or you who must take responsibility for this judgment, for it arises out of our interaction with our environment and entails the affirmation of the general reliability of our cognitive capacities. As Michael Polanyi puts it:

> Hence to accept the framework of commitment as the only situation in which sincere affirmations can be made, is to accredit in advance (if anything is ever to be affirmed) affirmations against which objections can be

raised that cannot be refuted. It allows us to commit ourselves on evidence which, but for the weight of our own personal judgment, would admit of other conclusions. We may firmly believe what we might conceivably doubt; and may hold to be true what might conceivably be false.[11]

Here again, someone might ask, What has all this to do with the definition of or the criteria for knowledge? My answer is that since it is *we*, as individual knowing subjects, who set definitions and criteria in accord with our tasks and intentions, these standards must never be described as if they exist and function independently of these activities and purposes. Moreover, they must not be employed as if they could be disengaged from the persons who define and set them in the first place, and whose ongoing cognitive activity continues to legitimize them. Modern epistemology, especially in its contemporary manifestations, has been guilty of such confusions.

To bring all this home, when the concept of knowledge is mired in such "objectivity" confusions, it is all too easy to dismiss the notion of transcendence as entirely subjective and noncognitive in character. The strictures of logical rules and notations leave no room for paradoxical and metaphorical assertions, modes of speech more appropriate to the expression of a *dimensional* reality. In like manner, the reductionism entailed by an empiricist analysis of experience in terms of observational propositions systematically eliminates the possibility of an awareness of a *mediated* reality. On the other hand, the acknowledgment of the personal quality of all cognitive activity enables us to construe knowledge in such a way as to allow, indeed to require, a more open-textured understanding of reality. This opens the way to a more viable notion of transcendence as dimensional and mediated.

We have been considering the personal dimension of the knowing process. It is time now to consider its balancing counterpart, the social dimension. For, it must be remembered that all human activity, including and especially the cognitive enterprise, takes place within the fabric of social reality. Thus, all the previous distinctions must be interpreted as applying to persons involved in a common, interrelational form of life, not to isolated individuals. Almost the entire history of Western intellectual history, whether philosophical or theological, has been carried on and written as if ideas and theories were developed by conceptual Robinson

---

[11]Polanyi, *Personal Knowledge* (New York: Harper & Row, 1958) 312.

Crusoes who only reported their efforts to one another ex post facto. This atomism has been responsible for much epistemological distortion, as has the impersonalism I have already examined.

It is helpful to think of the personal and the social aspects of human cognitive experience as forming two interdependent poles of a common continuum. In certain senses and instances they work against each other, the individual standing over against the traditions and conclusions of the group, challenging and reforming them. At the same time, however, the two can only be said to function in relation to each other, since the group is composed of individuals, and individuals would not come into being without the group. In short, the dynamic of this continuum is symbiotic in nature, and it can be thought of as having three main levels or dimensions: the ontological, the historical, and the sociological.

The speakers of language, namely persons, factor into cognitive experience as a fundamental aspect of social reality at the basic ontological level. The so-called problem of other minds, like Zeno's famous paradoxes, is only a problem for professional philosophers. All members of the human community, including such philosophers, begin relating to others as persons from the outset. As P. F. Strawson has shown, the notion of person is "logically primitive" in all natural languages, and as M. Merleau-Ponty has shown, it is "ontologically primordial" to our shared embodied existence. We do not first know ourselves and then come to know other persons by an inferential process. Rather, we begin by relating to others as persons, through embodiment and speech, and come to know ourselves thereby.

What constitutes knowledge is also subject to social processes of a historical nature. The idea that we stockpile knowledge, as so many hunks of information and fact, is an illusion created by the cult of objectivity that separates the knower from the known and treats the latter as if it can exist independently of the knowing process. Fortunately, this illusion has been put pretty much to rest in recent years by the likes of N. R. Hanson and Thomas Kuhn.[12] It is now becoming clear that the history of scientific knowledge is not strictly progressive and accumulative, but is relative to the expectations and standards of various historical contexts.

The particular problems, techniques, and root metaphors of a given time and place largely determine the *theoretical framework*—the structure

---

[12]Thomas Kuhn, *The Structure of Scientific Revolutions* (Chicago: University of Chicago Press, 1970).

within which the projects and findings of what Kuhn calls "normal science" develop. When the problems and techniques change, or when the findings are increasingly difficult to harmonize with the theories, a crisis develops and in turn paves the way for what Kuhn terms a "scientific revolution"; then the theoretical framework itself is seriously modified or entirely replaced. The shift from the Ptolemaic to the Copernican way of modeling the solar system, as well as that from Newtonian to Einsteinian physics, illustrates how the "paradigm" underlying scientific activity, and thus the knowledge, of a given epoch can be altered by factors other than new information.

An awareness of the historical aspect in all knowing not only underscores the social character of both knowledge and truth, but it facilitates the implementation of the central concern of the present book: namely, a shifting of the philosophical and theological axis away from the deadlock between objectivism and subjectivism and toward a perspective that allows for the recovery of transcendence. In Kuhnian terminology, my aim is to highlight that the metaphysical and epistemological paradigms underlying modern thought, those of dualism and atomism, have outlived their usefulness and have created a major crisis with respect to the notion of transcendence. My proposal is a fresh paradigm, one that incorporates the possibility of transcendence into its dimensional, mediational, and relational structure.

The sociological aspect or the social character of knowledge is closely related to the historical. Here again, the point is to acknowledge that knowing does not take place in a vacuum, but in the context of human activity and institutions. Not only are linguistic and historical factors highly relevant and determinant, but the processes whereby these factors, along with individual efforts and findings, are incorporated and legitimated into the fabric of our common cognitive experience are especially crucial as well. After all, facts and knowledge do not simply turn up or grow on trees. There is a concrete sense in which they are *produced* by the sociopolitical systems of a given culture. Let us consider several ways in which this is so.

It often escapes the notice of those who are the most concerned with truth and knowledge that people do not go about uttering propositions as ends in themselves. We do not just *say* things such as "The cat is on the mat" or "This book is written in English" for their own sake. Rather, we say them in order to accomplish some *task* or to achieve some *effect*, such as getting someone to remove the cat or indicating how the book should be cataloged. Even if the most basic function of language is said to be the transfer of information, which it clearly is not, people do not communicate information willy-nilly; rather, we do so in order to get certain broader jobs done, to facilitate the business of life.

J. L. Austin's analysis of linguistic activity, in terms of "speech-acts" that accomplish several purposes simultaneously, goes right to the heart of the issues involved.[13] It is, after all, persons who speak. Thus, it is persons who are correct or incorrect in their judgments. Moreover, it is other persons to whom we speak and who ultimately decide what our statements mean and whether or not they are true. For we learn to speak and mean in interaction with others, and it is in and through such interaction that we mutually decide what is true and what is false. Nothing can meaningfully be affirmed as true which every other person appropriately involved denies. There is nothing arbitrary or conventional about this, since our conventions arise in the context of our common social and practical activity.

At the ontic level, in terms of "what there is," we are also crucially dependent on our participation in social practices and shared values. The realities that populate our world, or worlds, come into being for us in and through our interaction with others by means of established conventions, practices, and values. What we see, hear, feel, and think arises largely from within common group activity. The Eskimo, for instance, have no word for snow in general and thus do not "see" generic snow. They instead make at least thirty differentiations with regard to the depths, textures, densities of the surface of their environment; thus they "see" more than thirty kinds of snow. In like manner, people who live in jungles hear and smell unseen things that we would never hear or smell, let alone see. The Tasaday tribe in the Philippines has no words for, no experience of aggression or of the difficulties of adolescence, while we do not— as they do—fear eclipses and the spirits of the dead.

All of these variations, as well as the more common, everyday similarities amongst people, are a result of our enculturation into the practices and commitments constituting the human way of being in the world. They are a function of our interaction with what G. H. Mead termed the "significant others" in our lives. Mead summarizes this insight in the following manner:

> Of course we are not only what is common to all: each one of the selves is
> different from everyone else; but there has to be such a common structure

---

[13]J. L. Austin, *How to Do Things with Words* (Cambridge: Harvard University Press, 1962).

as I have sketched in order that we may be members of a community at all. We cannot be ourselves unless we are also members in whom there is a community of attitudes which control the attitudes of all. We cannot have rights unless we have common attitudes. That which we have acquired as self-conscious persons makes us members of society and gives us selves. Selves can only exist in definite relationships to other selves. No hard-and-fast line can be drawn between our own selves and the selves of others, since our own selves exist and enter as such into our experience only insofar as the selves of others exist and enter as such into our experience also. The individual possesses a self only in relation to the selves of the other members of his social group; and the structure of his self expresses or reflects the general behavior pattern of this social group to which he belongs, just as does the structure of the self of every other individual belonging to this social group.[14]

At the conceptual level of what Peter Berger has called the "sociology of knowledge," the role of sociopolitical processes is equally evident. The systems and procedures by means of which we legitimize or instantiate various theories and propositions as "facts" and "knowledge" play a far more important epistemic function than our traditional way of thinking about such matters allows us to see, much less admit. In an important sense, though not in an exclusive sense, what comes to be accepted as knowledge within any cultural and historical context is constituted by the sociopolitical practices relevant thereunto. This point is well made in a book by Peter Berger and Thomas Luckman entitled *The Social Construction of Reality*. Here is how they summarize this general theme:

> Language provides the fundamental superimposition of logic on the objectivated social world. The edifice of legitimations is built upon language and uses language as its principal instrumentality. The "logic" thus attributed to the institutional order is part of the socially available stock of knowledge and taken for granted as such. Since the well-socialized individual "knows" that his social world is a consistent whole, he will be constrained to explain both its functioning and malfunctioning in terms of this "knowledge."[15]

---

[14]G. H. Mead, *On Social Psychology* (Chicago: University of Chicago Press, 1956) 227.

[15]Peter Berger and Thomas Luckman, *The Social Construction of Reality* (New York: Doubleday, 1967) 64.

In the above remarks I cautioned that these social processes do not "exclusively" determine the content of knowledge; there is also a certain intractable character to reality that resists more conventional manipulation. Even as the sculptor must accommodate his or her creation to the limitations inherent within the chosen medium, so the knowledge we corporately "construct" remains partly a function of factors beyond our control. It is this acknowledgment that enables the relational understanding of knowledge to avoid the charge of relativism in general, and keeps the title and theme of Berger's and Luckman's book from being divested of all truth value. For, if truth is merely "where you find it," then even this cannot be "true." Even as Polanyi's notion of "universal intent" guards against absolute relativism and convention alone, so what he terms the social character of the epistemological enterprise guards against the absolutization of any particular knowledge claim or theoretical perspective. The social dimension of the quest for knowledge is not a *sufficient* condition thereof, but it most assuredly is a *necessary* one. Polanyi's following remarks put the point well.

> While compulsion by force or by neurotic obsession excludes responsibility, compulsion by universal intent establishes responsibility. The strain of this responsibility is the greater—other things being equal—the wider the range of alternatives left open to choice and the more conscientious the person responsible for the decision. While the choices in question are open to arbitrary egocentric decisions, a craving for the universal sustains a constructive effort and narrows down this discretion to the point where the agent making the decision finds that he cannot do otherwise. The freedom of the subjective person to do as he pleases is overruled by the freedom of the responsible person to act as he must.[16]

Once again it is important to connect these points to the notion of transcendence. If knowledge is construed in terms of a static state of a disembodied mind, induced by a passive exposure to objective truth that exists independently of that mind, then the prospects for a viable concept of transcendence are indeed dim. For, it is well-nigh impossible to establish the possibility, let alone the actuality, of perceptual knowledge using this model, to say nothing of the knowledge of persons, values, and relationships. The transcendent character inherent in these latter cognitions will go entirely undiscerned and unaccounted for if knowledge is

---

[16]Polanyi, *Personal Knowledge* (1958) 309.

restricted to such a one-dimensional model. Thus, that which is transcendent in the religious sense will be negated altogether.

On the other hand, when the personal and social aspects of the knowing experience are united with the tacit and embodied aspects, a mediational structure is provided for acknowledging a multidimensional transcendence *within* the entire range of cognitive awareness, including and especially the religious dimension. Discernment of the divine is now placed on equal logical footing with our awareness of the other experiential dimension constituting the worlds within which we exist and operate. The dualisms endemic to the traditional Western model—between the natural and the supernatural on the one hand and between the knower and the known on the other—have been eliminated, thereby clearing the way for a fresh understanding of the cognition of the transcendent.

4. Justification and Participation

We come now to the specifically epistemic question inherent in the forgoing sections of this chapter: on what basis are we to decide whether or not a specific knowledge claim is justified, and in particular, how are claims to a knowledge of transcendence to be settled? I shall begin with a brief presentation of the dominant modern model for adjudicating such questions, as focused in the work of Roderick Chisholm.

Taking his cue from Plato's *Meno* and *Theaetetus*, Professor Chisholm sets forth three conditions that must be met in order to distinguish "knowledge" from "true opinion."[17] These conditions may be said to serve as the defining characteristics of knowledge and have been adopted as such by an extremely large number of English-speaking philosophers. When we say that a given person (s) *knows* that a particular proposition (h) is true, we mean (1) that s *believes* that h, (2) that h is *true*, and (3) that h is *evident* for s.[18] The majority of Chisholm's efforts are devoted to working out the refinements and ramifications of this third condition; namely, what does it mean to say that a proposition is evident? The problems of empirical and logical truth, probability and analyticity, and sense data and

---

[17]Roderick Chisholm, *Theory of Knowledge* (New York: Prentice-Hall, 1966). I am using the first edition of Chisholm's book because it more clearly focuses the issue with which I am concerned. That the second edition (1976) makes no substantial change vis-à-vis the points I am making can be seen by examining its pages 102-18.

[18]Ibid., 5-23.

other methods all receive due attention. The chief conclusion is, however, that knowledge means "justified true belief."

Throughout his discussion Chisholm assumes that the third condition (h being evident for s) refers to "something," which when it is "added
to true opinion, the result is knowledge."[19] He terms this added ingre-
dient "a state," presumably a mental state, "that may be described or reported by means of the word 'know.' " By specifying the three conditions
that, when fulfilled, justify the use of the term *knowledge* as the proper
description of the subject-in-question's state, Chisholm has laid down
what he takes to be the foundations of epistemological endeavor.

My primary concern with Chisholm's way of defining knowledge
centers not in the viability of the third condition, but rather in the far-too-
quickly-glossed-over second condition. It seems somehow circular to define knowledge as that which is, among other things, true. For, this would
mean that in order to determine whether a given person's belief deserves
to be called knowledge we must, in addition to determining whether or
not it is a *justified* belief, be able to establish that it is *true*. The problem is
that the only way to ascertain whether or not a particular belief is true is
to evaluate certain knowledge claims on the basis of the justifications offered for them. There is no litmus test for truth. In short, in the standard
approach, knowledge is defined in terms of truth and truth is defined in
terms of justified knowledge claims or beliefs. Each is understood and
achieved by means of the other.

Now, of course, the standard reply to this way of putting things is that
it involves a failure to distinguish between the *definition* of knowledge and
the *test* for knowledge. It is generally claimed that the three formal *conditions* for determining whether *any* person rightfully can be said to know
that a given proposition is true must not be confused with the various
means that we necessarily employ in determining whether *a particular* person can be said to know any specific proposition. The definition of
knowledge, it is said, pertains to the *meaning* of the concept, while the
test for knowledge pertains to the *veracity* of a knowledge claim. Thus,
the reply goes, there is nothing circular about defining knowledge in terms
of what is true.

At this juncture, at least two responses suggest themselves. First, it
remains the case that the three formal criteria of knowledge are offered
as conditions that, when fulfilled, "yield knowledge," or allow us to say

---

[19]Ibid., 15.

that a given person (s) is in the "state of knowing." But, if we must determine whether or not these conditions have been met in order to be able to say that knowledge obtains, then it follows that establishing the *truth* of the proposition in question (h) must *precede* deciding whether or not the person who believes this proposition, even justifiably, can be said to *know* it. In short, before one can be said to know something we must determine whether or not it is true, which means we must know *that* they know.

Moreover, this knowledge (h^1) that what is known (h) is true must also be established on the basis of the three conditions for knowledge set forth as the defining characteristics of knowledge. Thus, determining the truth of h^1 must precede establishing whether or not it is knowledge—or whether or not the person (s) believing it is in the knowledge "state." In other words, we must know (h^2) that we know h^1 before it can be said that s knows h. Clearly, we have become involved in an infinite regress that makes it impossible ever to know anything, since the necessary condition for knowledge can never be satisfied.

Perhaps this infinite regress can be avoided if we refrain from speaking of the three criteria as conditions and speak of them exclusively as defining characteristics. Then they do not have to be fulfilled by anyone in practice, but only must be the case in principle. This brings us to the second of my responses mentioned above. Those who reason in this fashion, and Chisholm is a fair representative, do so in a manner which implies that it is possible to distinguish between principle and practice, between concept and activity without philosophical difficulty. Actually, it is this very assumption, which has plagued us at least since Plato's time, that generates rather than avoids philosophical difficulty. To speak of the truth of a given proposition as being fulfilled in an abstract, formal sense—as if this had no connection with the actual practice of determining concrete truths from falsehoods—is to create the illusion that epistemology is not a human activity.

There are at least two different ways of exposing this illusion. On the one hand, it is ultimately impossible to talk of knowledge and truth as if they stood beyond human experience and language without obscuring our understanding of them. For, even the distinction between the formal and material levels, between definitions and practices, is a distinction made by human minds and speech. In the final analysis, knowledge and truth are aspects of human experience and result from human activity. It is, of course, helpful to distinguish between "Truth" with uppercase letters and "truth" with lowercase letters in order to acknowledge the relative and finite character of all human epistemological endeavor in contrast to the ultimate, godlike perspective envisioned by LaPlace, toward which we aim. But clearly, such a formal ideal is irrelevant as a characteristic of knowledge as we experience it. It serves as a "regulative idea" to remind us of our limitations, but it makes no positive or material contribution to our search for knowledge.

Acknowledging the human element, or "personal coefficient," in all aspects of epistemological activity in no wise opens the door to subjectivism or skepticism. Rather, it simply enables us to accredit the individual powers and social processes by means of which we make knowledge claims in the first place and by means of which we confirm or disconfirm them. The real issue with knowledge claims is in what sense and to what degree they should and can be justified. To add to this the condition that they must also be true is to spin a conceptual fifth wheel that generates unnecessary philosophical difficulties. We can easily acknowledge both that we aim at an absolute, unchanging perspective on reality and that we as humans always fall short of this ideal without reifying truth into Truth, à la Heidegger vis-à-vis "Nothing."

On the other hand, this illusion that truth somehow exists apart from and can be defined independently of human cognitive activity may be exposed by noting that our concepts and our practices are symbiotic in nature. We construct and acquire our concepts of truth and knowledge, as we do all our notions, from within the give-and-take of our interactions with the world and each other. To define knowledge in terms of truth, as if this concept stood on its own (both formally and practically) is to perpetuate epistemological confusion. What we mean by truth is to a large degree a function of our everyday cognitive activity.

To say that s knows that h because, in addition to *believing* it and being *justified* in so believing, h is *true* flies in the face of the fact that truth itself is a human notion that only takes on meaning in *relation* to cognitive claims, processes, and procedures. We judge belief in h as knowledge if it is, among other things, true; but we also judge whether h is true by the same activities that we engage in to ascertain if s's believing h is a case of knowledge. In other words, at best adding "h being true" to the defining characteristics of "h being knowledge" is a fine example of language idling, while at worst it conjures up transcendent yet inaccessible realities.

As Wittgenstein makes clear, this approach does not lead to conventionalism, since at the bedrock level what we say and do on the one hand and what is real and true for us on the other hand are inextricably interwoven.[20] Human patterns of thought and speech are neither arbitrary nor fixed. They are true because they work and they work because they are true; it is useless to haggle about which is more fundamental. Some have called this "linguistic pragmatism," which is acceptable so long as we acknowledge that we are talking of language at its deepest level, as the matrix of all thought and speech.

When we state some of the things we know, or when we can be said to know certain things even though we have not said that we do, what is accomplished by calling this "a description of a state"? Surely this conjures up a process of introspection parallel to an empirical description of our surroundings, and just as surely nothing of this sort is involved. What is gained from an epistemological point of view, since the reality and nature of such a state play no part in the tasks in which we are commonly engaged? If I say that I know the way to San Jose, you are not concerned with my cognitive "state" but with being directed there. And if I claim not to know the way to get us there, of what use is it to talk of "states of cognizance"? Thus, "I know" and the like do not describe so much as indicate, warrant, and guide, as Austin claimed.

On the contrary, what we *do* mean when we say that another person knows something is simply that when put to the test, that person can tell us or show us what it is we want to know. Whether speaking of another's knowledge or of our own, we are participating in a public activity that gets its life not from describing internal states, but from the give-and-take of everyday life. Proof of this is that questions concerning the veracity of our knowledge claims are not settled by reference to whether or not we are in a particular state (how on earth would we settle such questions?), but by acting on these claims in various ways and paying attention to the outcome.

The final line of argument offered on behalf of the standard definition of knowledge is often put this way. That being true must be one of the defining characteristics of knowledge, in addition to being believed and being justified, is shown by the simple fact that if a given justified belief turns out to be *untrue*, we say the person whose belief it was did *not know*. If s believes h and has good reason to do so, but h turns out to be false, then s cannot be said to have known that h. In other words, to be justified in using the word *know*, we must be unable to be wrong. If we say we know something and it turns out otherwise, we did not know and should

---

[20]Cf. Barry Stroud, "Wittgenstein and Logical Necessity," *Philosophical Review* 74:4 (October 1965): 504-18.

not have said that we know. Thus, being true is essential to the meaning of the concept of knowledge.

I contend that the above account of knowledge conflates two quite separate issues. The issues are (1) whether or not *being* true is a necessary condition for a belief to qualify as knowledge and (2) whether or not a person has the right to *say* he or she knows if the belief in question has not yet been established as true. Now we must move carefully here. The standard account, when its proponents have been made aware that there are in fact two issues involved, might be revised so as to settle the second question on the basis of the first. If being true is taken as a prerequisite for a belief's qualifying as knowledge, then clearly we should never claim to know until it has been established that our belief is true. There are, however, two fatal difficulties with this approach.

To begin with, such a requirement for the use of the term *know* is unduly inflationary. For, it clearly would prohibit the making of knowledge claims concerning a great deal of what we always have said and must be able to say that we know. This definition of knowledge prices it off the market. Moreover, the establishment of the truth of a given belief is itself part of the process of justifying that belief, not a separate condition that can be determined independently. We establish the truth of a claim by examining the evidence, empirical or logical, for it, and this is the same as determining whether or not the claim is justified. Thus, what we mean when we say that a given belief turns out to be untrue, and therefore that it should not have been or be called knowledge, is that further evidence now indicates that the belief is not justified. Determining the truth or falsity of a given belief is not an additional step to that of determining whether or not it is a justified belief.

One is justified in making a knowledge claim when and only when the situation, including the evidence, warrants it. Nothing else is required, because any other conditions turn out to be aspects of this very warranting process. If and when further factors indicate that the claim is not warranted, then one no longer is justified in making it. No special feat of transcendent truth knowing or guarantee that one cannot be mistaken is required in order for a person to have the right to claim that he knows something to be the case.

In conclusion, then, the only proper definition of knowledge is simply "justified belief." A person can claim to know whenever he or she is in a position to do so, that is, when the proper contextual conditions are fulfilled and when the evidence warrants it. When additional information indicates that these factors do not obtain, then knowledge cannot be claimed. To stipulate the additional condition that what the person affirms must also "be the case" is to confuse the issue either by (1) launching an infinite regress, (2) requiring what cannot possibly be supplied, or (3) reaffirming what has already been asked for. We are entitled to make knowledge claims when our beliefs are justified, no more and no less.

The crucial issue is not the definition of knowledge, but when we are justified in saying that we or someone else "knows" something. We are not so justified when we have determined that what is being claimed is beyond any question "the case." Rather, we are so justified when sufficient grounds are present to render such a claim beyond reasonable doubt in the given context. For, establishing that what is claimed is the case ("that P") ultimately collapses into the question of justification. We withdraw the claim not when it has been proven that reality does not correspond to it, but when the grounds no longer are adequate. Adequate justification is both necessary *and* sufficient to warrant a knowledge claim. What we mean by saying that P must obtain—in addition to believing that P and having good grounds for doing so—is simply that when adequate grounds are not or are no longer present, we withhold the term *knowledge*. That this is all we could mean by such a statement is shown by asking: after we have considered the relevant evidential factors, what is there left to do in addition? To ask if P is the case is the *same thing* as to ask if we have grounds for believing it.

Largely on the basis of a Chisholmian definition of knowledge, modern philosophy has rejected all claims to knowledge of the transcendent, since they can never be shown to be "true." Under the light provided by the above reconstruction of the concept of knowledge, however, such rejection is no longer necessary or even possible. Claims to knowledge of a transcendent, religious dimension of experienced reality, as mediated in and through the other dimensions, are now on equal footing with all cognitive claims. They stand or fall based on the degree to which they are or can be justified or confirmed within the broad scope and depth of human experience. Moreover, since such claims will be primarily tacit in character, as befits mediated knowledge, determining their degree of confirmation will be a difficult and relatively open-ended process at best. Nevertheless, the viability of such claims, and thus the possibility of transcendence itself, has now been established in principle. Individual claims to knowledge of the transcendent must needs be taken up one at a time.

Four

DOING:

Value

as Relational and Contextual

If reality can be said to constitute the broadest and deepest context within which human existence takes place, then it might be said that within this context we exist at the intersection of three main modes of being: (1) knowing, (2) doing, and (3) saying. After having discussed the dimensional and mediational character of reality in chapter 2, as well as the interactive and tacit quality of knowing in chapter 3, it remains for us to consider the modes of doing and saying in this and the subsequent chapter, respectively. While it might be going too far to say that these three modes of being exhaust the reality of human existence, I do believe that they provide an adequate schema within which to treat the essential aspects of the human way of being in the world.

1. The Vertical and the Horizontal

In classical and medieval thought moral values were grounded in the transcendent. Prior to the modern era, both philosophy and theology looked to some notion of that which is "beyond" or "other than" human and natural reality as the source of moral standards. In modern times the tendency has been to seek a strictly human and/or natural grounding for morality. This has produced a great deal more difficulty in the theological realm than the philosophical, since the idea of a naturalistic or humanistic religion has never quite convinced the majority of those who take religious belief seriously. The contemporary world has acquired this bifurcated legacy, but as yet has been unable to make peace with it.

In his provocative book *After Virtue*, Alasdair MacIntyre focuses this shift of emphasis, along with its ensuing contemporary confusion, by contrasting the moral theories of Aristotle and Nietzsche.[1] He argues that whereas the former, and traditional morality with him, stressed the crucial role of character in the grounding of ethical value, the latter, and modern morality as well, stressed the autonomy of individual will. It is helpful to characterize the difference between traditional and modern value theory as involving a shift from a vertical to a horizontal emphasis. Classical philosophers had a strong tendency to ground moral values metaphysically in the structure of ultimate reality. The more other-worldly thinkers—such as Pythagoras, Parmenides, and Plato—spoke of the unchanging reality of mathematical relationships, Being itself, and the Forms, respectively. The more this-worldly thinkers—such as Aristotle, the Stoics, and Epicurus—sought a balancing of the patterns and processes constituting the all-encompassing cosmos. Only the Sophists and Skeptics denied the viability of such metaphysical grounding for moral virtue.

Medieval theologians followed suit, seeking accommodation with one or the other of these two classical traditions. Augustine adapted the Platonic posture to that of the Christian Scriptures, viewing the Forms as constituting the mind of God and the Form of the Good as God. Aquinas took the other tack, building his understanding of Christian faith on the precepts of Aristotle. Thus, some moral virtues were said to be based in human nature and reason, while others were taken to be based in the divine nature and revelation. In either case, however, the primary thrust of moral theory until the rise of the modern period in the seventeenth century was vertical in direction.

Modern philosophy has shifted the basis of moral theory to the horizontal dimension. Here, too, there are two main emphases—the naturalistic and the humanistic. The former emphasis—represented by such thinkers as Hobbes, Spinoza, and Nietzsche—focused on morality as an expression of the basic principles inherent in the regular processes of the natural world. Pain, pleasure, reason, and growth, as the built-in regulators of human life, were said to be sufficient guides for the value decisions that we face in daily life. The more humanistic emphasis in modern

---

[1] Alasdair MacIntyre, *After Virtue* (Notre Dame: University of Notre Dame Press, 1984).

value theory—represented by the likes of Locke, Kant, and J. S. Mill—stressed social responsibility as the basis of morality. The notions of social contract, "kingdom of ends in themselves," and utilitarianism were set forth as the key to the moral life.

In the modern era the theological approach to moral value became a bit more confused. On the one hand, it was increasingly difficult to maintain the transcendent or vertical perspective in light of the critiques leveled against it by both naturalists and humanists. On the other hand, it required a great deal of courage and creativity to seek a horizontal basis for religious value theory. The Thomistic tradition, in both its Catholic and Anglican modes, strove to remain true to the vertical perspective while dealing honestly with the challenge of modernism. Other thinkers, more Protestant in character, made bold attempts to reinterpret religious morality in terms of the new, horizontal perspective. Friedrich Schleiermacher and Ludwig Feuerbach are two of the more impressive examples of this latter approach. Nevertheless, it is generally concluded that such efforts necessarily relinquished the possibility of genuine transcendence in the process of accommodation.

In the twentieth century, the question of the bases of moral value has been essentially dismissed. On their side, the logical empiricists have denied the cognitive significance of value judgments in general, arguing that they are merely expressions of feelings or desires. On the other side, existentialists have reduced morality to a function of individual decision making as an expression of radical freedom and authenticity in the face of absurdity and nothingness. A. J. Ayer and Charles Stevenson are prime examples of that "emotivist-imperativist" emphasis of logical empiricism, while Jean-Paul Sartre and Martin Heidegger exemplify the existentialist perspective. In spite of their many disagreements, these two dominant philosophical movements of the twentieth century agree that no transcendent basis for morality is either possible or necessary.

In the context of such stark "horizontalism" on the philosophical scene, religious moral theorists have taken a variety of positions. Some, such as Karl Barth and his followers, have flatly denied all attempts to reduce religious morality to any form of human reason or feeling, insisting instead that true moral responsibility derives exclusively from one's relation to the divine as transcending the human realm. Others, such as R. M. Hare and R. B. Braithwaite, have been willing to accept the reduction of all religious statements to the level of expressions of human sentiments and commitments. Still others, such as Paul Tillich and Reinhold Niebuhr,

have sought to incorporate the existentialist perspective into their interpretation of religious ethics.

Among all these variations, the notion of transcendence gets lost in
the shuffle. Stoutly to affirm the vertical understanding, together with its
accompanying metaphysical dualism, is increasingly difficult and unproductive, while to accommodate the horizontal point of view renders religious moral values both irrelevant and shallow. What is needed is an
understanding of moral transcendence that allows for a grounding of
ethical values in something more than mere nature and/or humanity, but
which at the same time incorporates these latter dimensions in a helpful
and realistic manner. The skeleton of such an understanding has been
presented in the previous chapters. It remains, now, to flesh out this
skeleton into a more concrete ethical theory.

Before moving on to this important task, one further preliminary step
is in order. Some attention must be given to more recent developments
in philosophical moral theory. In particular, I have in mind the contributions of those thinkers who have constructed a perspective that focuses on "the moral point of view," on the one hand, and those who have
stressed the role of "good reasons" in providing a basis for ethical judgments, on the other. These developments provide valuable clues to the
structure of a relational and contextual understanding of the transcendent basis of morality.

Amid the discussion of whether or not moral judgments can be given
any grounding whatsoever—a discussion instigated by the skeptical critique of all ethical theory since the collapse of classical and medieval transcendentalism—a perspective has been developed that emphasizes the
primordial character of moral reasoning. Against those who have argued
that "since God is dead, anything is permitted," certain philosophers have
insisted that not only is morality possible apart from some metaphysical
and/or theological grounding, but it can be shown that it is necessary to
the human way of being in the world. The claim is that to be a member
of the human community is to participate in life from "the moral point of
view," even when one questions the very basis and possibility of morality.

Kurt Baier is an excellent representative of this approach, and his
thinking can be summarized in the following way.[2] To participate in morality is to engage in asking for and giving reasonable justification for our

---

[2]Kurt Baier, *The Moral Point of View* (New York: Random House, 1965).

conduct. When asked "why did you do that?" in a moral context, a person is expected to supply a reason that will be acceptable to the others who are participating in that general context. Moreover, to ask "why" in such situations is a form of participation, since asking itself constitutes a deed within this form of life. Even to ask, "Why should we give reasons for our conduct?" is to indicate one's participation in the moral point of view. A broader form of this argument seeks to point out that the general activity of asking for and giving reasons is constitutive of being human. Thus, even to ask for reasons why one would give reasons, for a rationale for being rational, is itself a form of rationality. In other words, one is already participating in the activity one seeks to question when one questions the viability of the question-asking activity in general.

The conclusion to be drawn here is that somehow the moral point of view is part of the very makeup of human nature; it neither can be given nor needs any justification outside itself. In a certain sense this approach is both naturalistic and humanistic at the same time, thus making it possible to classify it as a horizontal, nontranscendent view of the nature of moral value. On the other hand, it is also possible to see this general approach as providing a means of slipping between the horns of the vertical-horizontal dilemma and developing a way of grounding moral values that is at once transcendent without being otherworldly. It is this possibility, one that is congruent with the overall proposal of this present book, with which the following sections of this chapter will be concerned.

Another development in contemporary moral theory that is pertinent to the task of finding a way to preserve transcendence with respect to values is the "good reasons" approach to moral justification. The background here is the familiar debate as to whether moral judgments are absolute or relative. Clearly, there are connections between this discussion and that of the contrast between the vertical and horizontal grounding of moral judgments. In general, those who hold to the view that a vertical or transcendent grounding is both necessary and possible tend to be those who maintain that such grounding is absolute, while those of the horizontal persuasion are usually more open to the idea of moral relativity. A sufficient number of exceptions exist to indicate that these two discussions must be treated separately. Kant's horizontal "absolutism" and Aristotle's vertical "relativism" are two cases in point.

Against those who maintain that moral judgments must be absolute in order to be viable, which includes both absolutists and relativists, those who advocate the "good reasons" approach argue that a contextual justification is all that is necessary.[3] In any given moral situation, the factors and persons involved provide sufficient criteria for determining whether an act is moral or not. There is no need to establish an ultimate basis for moral judgments when a contextual one will do. Generally, for example, an act of violence is accepted as justified if it can be established that it was done in self-defense. The agreement of those involved is sufficient to terminate the search for further grounding.

It is possible to broaden any given context by asking whether the agreement reached therein is itself justified; however, once again, this question is settled by those involved in the discussion on the basis of their agreement. Of course, such agreement may not always be forthcoming, but this only means that the search for some basis of agreement must continue if a stalemate, or worse, is to be avoided. This contextualist perspective only requires that "good reasons" or sufficient reasons, not ultimate reasons, be given for a moral judgment. In other words, it is both possible and adequate to ground moral justifications in something other than absolute standards, namely in the context of common tasks, commitments, and agreements.

If it is possible to settle questions of morality contextually, thus avoiding both absolutism and relativism, then it would seem possible to speak of morality having a grounding that transcends mere subjectivism and conventionalism without viewing this grounding as existing independently of the decisions and valuations of those involved. To put this insight in the vocabulary of Michael Polanyi, the acknowledgment of the "universal intent" in all moral judgments bears witness to a transcendent dimension in moral activity, while the acknowledgment of the sociopolitical dimension guards against the temptation to equate any given set of moral standards with that transcendent dimension. Moral skepticism and relativism, like their counterparts in epistemology, are avoided by means of a contextualist approach that stresses the adequacy of good reasons while abandoning the demand for ultimate reasons. Moral arrogance, like its epistemological parallel, is also avoided by contextualism, since it allows for a continuous broadening of the context of moral discourse without ever claiming to have "arrived."

------

[3]See, e.g., Stephen Toulmin's *An Examination of the Place of Reason in Ethics* (London: Cambridge University Press, 1950).

2. Context and Responsibility

The most helpful way to develop a contextualist moral theory is to focus on the notion of responsibility, rather than on questions of absolutism and relativism. To start out searching for or denying the existence of an ultimate foundation for moral judgment is wrong-headed because it causes us to overlook the actual process of moral discourse and justification itself. Just what happens when people seek to determine what they should do in a moral situation? How is moral responsibility understood and established? I maintain that as participants in the moral point of view, we seek good or sufficient reasons, rather than ultimate reasons, for our judgments.

In his extremely profound book *The Responsible Self,* H. Richard Niebuhr has given an excellent exploration of the factors constituting the warp and weft of responsibility.[4] Niebuhr begins by defining responsibility in terms of the answer we give to the question, What is the fitting thing to do in response to what we perceive to be our concrete moral situation? He suggests that the responsible person does not first ask "what is the *right* thing to do?" answering in terms of duty, nor "what is the *good* thing to do?" answering in terms of ends and means. Rather, according to Niebuhr, the responsible person seeks to determine the appropriate course of action in light of the circumstances.

While seeking the response that best fits the context, a responsible agent will, of course, consider the deontological and teleological perspectives, but they will always function as factors within the analysis, rather than as its conclusion. In extreme cases, the right and the good may turn out *not* to be the most *appropriate* response. In a theological framework, this three-way distinction is usually cast in terms of the Law of God (deontological duty) and the Will of God (teleological goals) on the one side and "situationalism" on the other.

Niebuhr's contextualism runs much deeper, however, than situationalism. Indeed, his analysis of the factors involved goes far beyond "doing the loving thing." In addition to acknowledging that one's response to a situation requires individual interpretation, the responsible person is also aware that in responding, rather than simply reacting, one will be accountable in the sense that other persons in turn will be responding to this particular response. Thus a responsible moral action will be part of a

[4]H. R. Niebuhr, *The Responsible Self* (New York: Harper & Row, 1963).

broad pattern of behavior in human relationships across time. It is this notion of historical and social continuity that distinguishes Niebuhr's contextualism from situationalism.

The responsible person will reflect upon and anticipate such questions as: *Who* will be affected and *how? Why* would I prefer this response to that one? How and why will *I* be affected by the responses of others to my response? *Seeking* answers to such questions is itself a manifestation of responsibility, according to Niebuhr, even if the answers of various individuals do not agree. Thus, for the contextualist, responsibility is more a function of posture and procedure than one of standards and answers. *How* one goes about making a moral judgment is more determinative of responsibility than *what* one decides.

Throughout his entire analysis, Niebuhr relies heavily on what he calls the "social character of selfhood." According to Niebuhr, individual moral agents do not arrive on the scene and function as isolated and self-contained Leibnizian "monads," but come into being and continue to operate as *relational* persons bound together by their participation in their social environment. This emphasis in Niebuhr's work dovetails nicely with the "symbolic interactionism" of G. H. Mead. The self is not best conceived of atomistically, but organismically, as an intersection of a variety of processes and encounters.

> To be a self in the presence of other selves is not a derivative experience but primordial. To be able to say that I am I is not an inference from the statement that I think thoughts nor from the statement that I have a law-acknowledging conscience. It is, rather, the acknowledgement of my existence as the counterpart of another self. The exploration of this dimension of self-existence has taken place in many areas of modern man's thinking; many lines of inquiry have converged on the recognition that the self is fundamentally social, in this sense that it is a being which not only knows itself in relation to other selves but exists as self only in that relation.[5]

The significance of the social character of selfhood for a contextualist moral theory is at least threefold. First, the distinction between individual and corporate responsibility must be understood as far more complex than is commonly thought. Not only are the social conditions out of which one comes exceedingly important in determining just where and to what degree responsibility lies, but the relationships in which one is currently

---

[5]Ibid., 71.

involved become highly significant as well. This is one of the reasons why there is an increasing tendency, for example, to include family members and close friends, as well as coworkers, in various forms of psychological therapy. The more organic, as contrasted to mechanical, a phenomenon is, the more contextual and relational factors must be taken into account.

Second, when a person seeks to act responsibly as a social self, the range of relevant persons and considerations is greatly expanded. As one who is inextricably connected to "significant others" and societal institutions, a moral agent not only decides and acts for him- or herself, but does so for others as well. The so-called consequences of one's actions are not merely *results* thereof, but are part and parcel of the acts themselves. When I promise something to or lie to another person, I am not simply affecting him, I am engaging him and thereby incorporating him into my act as well. Moral behavior is not performed on a stage and received passively by others, rather, moral behavior resembles more the steps and moves in an intricate folk dance engaged in by a close-knit community. In a deep sense, when we choose and act we do so for others as well, not as their representatives but as mutual participants in a shared form of life.

Third, the corporate nature of human selfhood factors into the responsible person's moral decision-making process in terms of the notion of accountability. The choices we make will be, in turn, responded to by others, both directly and indirectly as well as positively and negatively. Such responses will be anticipated by the responsible moral agent, so as to be incorporated into the rationale leading to a particular moral judgment. It is not possible to specify in advance exactly how such factors will influence one's decisions and behavior—that is, how much weight will be given to each and which will be positive or negative. Nonetheless, a responsible social-self will act with such things in mind, knowing that other persons are social and responsive agents as well.

Just what is the connection between a contextualist understanding of responsibility and the possibility of grounding moral values in a way that transcends relativism while avoiding traditional dualism? The connecting link between these two concerns is the general concept of mediation as it was employed in chapter 2. There reality was conceived of as a series of simultaneously interpenetrating dimensions, arranged according to a hierarchy of richness and comprehensiveness, each level of which is mediated in and through those that are less rich and comprehensive. Moreover, the latter set the boundary conditions within which and supply the necessary particulars by means of which the former become a part of experienced reality, even though they are themselves less significant. Finally, as suggested in chapter 3, those dimensions of reality that are the more mediated in nature can only be discerned interactively and tacitly, since they can neither be known directly nor inferentially.

One of the richer and more comprehensive dimensions of human experience is the moral or ethical. Thus, the concepts and insights, the disclosures and discernments that constitute the moral dimension are mediated in and through the particulars constituting the less rich and comprehensive dimensions of experience, such as the physical and the personal. Our moral awareness necessarily arises within our physical and personal experience, but it is by no means limited to them. In short, our moral awareness can indeed be said to transcend these other dimensions and the particulars of which they consist, without being said to exist prior to and/or independently of them.

Traditional dualism, or realmism, finds it necessary to define transcendence in terms of some realm or mode of reality that is in no way dependent on the less significant aspects of reality and experience. Thus, the only way to ground moral values transcendently is to establish them as absolute and unchanging. At the same time, modern naturalism and/or humanism finds it necessary to deny any transcendent basis for morality and thus to affirm relativism in order to allow the particulars of human historical and social existence their rightful significance. I assert that this dichotomy can be resolved by defining transcendence in terms of mediated dimensions, which are "more" than those by which they are mediated without being independent of them.

Obviously, such a proposal requires that each side in the current debate be prepared to negotiate certain key issues. Rather than perceive this process as one of compromise and trade-off, I would prefer to construe it as one of true synthesis, in the Hegelian sense. For in the notion of mediation the fundamental concern of both verticalism and horizontalism is fulfilled, while the particular forms in which they are cast are negated. They are both fulfilled in the sense that, on the dualist side, the mediated dimension is not reducible to the mediating dimensions, while, on the naturalist and/or humanist side, the mediated dimension is not viewed as independent of the mediating dimensions. Thus, both are fulfilled and negated, and in Hegel's term, they both are "transcended," no pun intended.

What matters here is that it is possible, with this notion of mediated transcendence, to have a grounding for moral value that goes beyond and deeper than a flat, horizontal perspective without featuring the dualism that renders morality "so heavenly-minded as to be of no earthly good." Values, like reality and knowledge, do not need to be defined as independent of *less* significant aspects of experience in order to be *more* significant than them. In addition, these latter aspects do not need to be all that there is in order to be significant in their own right. As G. E. Moore said, whenever someone tells us that A is "only" or "merely" B, we have a right to be suspicious. People initially distinguished between A and B for good reasons, and the burden of proof lies with those who would deny this distinction. Conversely, to say that A is "other" than B does not entail that it exists and functions independently of B. It is this insight that the notion of mediated transcendence seeks to safeguard.

Now, with specific reference to the importance and viability of a contextualist understanding of moral responsibility, what is needed is to connect up the notions of mediation and contextuality. The schematic connection between these two ideas should already be fairly obvious, since they both have played significant roles in the previous chapters. In mediation, that which is mediated discloses itself in and through the particular factors making up a given, concrete context. In a word, mediation is always contextual. On the other hand, a context is that in and through which a mediated disclosure is discerned; it is that which mediates. A context provides the juncture-point at and by which the significance of an event or phenomenon is grasped. In sum, mediation and context are symbiotic, both ontologically and epistemologically.

With regard to the grounding of moral value, then, we see the connection between these two crucial notions in more incarnate form. In the ethical dimension of existence, in the events and encounters, the quandaries and decisions of everyday moral life, the relationship between mediation and context is fleshed out. In the concentric contexts of our day-by-day beings and doings, we become aware of our responsibilities to one another in and through our relational interaction. These contexts mediate our responsibilities as more than mere conveniences and conventions, as grounded in a dimension of reality that transcends the contexts themselves. Nevertheless, our discernment of these responsibilities cannot take place apart from a thorough consideration and evaluation of such things as pleasure, pain, self-interest, social utility, "categorical imperatives," God's will, and the like. None or all of these factors are sufficient in determining moral conduct, but they are nonetheless necessary to this task.

This connection between context and mediated transcendence enables us to overcome the standard dichotomies between vertical and horizontal perspectives on the one hand and absolute and relative values on the other. For, we can now speak of moral values being grounded transcendently, in the sense of being discerned as mediated from a dimension that is more than the purely human and/or natural. At the same time, however, these values cannot be discerned apart from a thorough consideration of the human and natural factors forming the ethical context, since these constitute the medium through which moral values are mediated.

When placed within a theological framework, the forgoing considerations enable us to speak of God's moral will both transcendently and sociopolitically. It makes no sense, nor is it helpful, to speak of the divine will in the abstract—as if there exists a cosmic code of law that dictates what is right and wrong irrespective of the contexts within which we carry on our personal and social activity. Religious ethics are made relevant to the circumstances of life by being viewed as mediated in and through them, not by being thought of as delivered from above in hermetically sealed containers. Likewise, an exhaustive search of the historical and contextual factors of our personal and social activity will never provide an exhaustive religious grounding for our ethical values. The religious dimension must be discerned as that richer and more comprehensive dimension that encompasses and fills our less complex dimensions with meaning as it is disclosed within them.

A question now remains as to how the notion of mediated transcendence, as the ground of moral responsibility, actually works itself out in the push-and-pull of contextual activity. What is it that keeps ethical norms from becoming ossified and irrelevant on the one hand or amorphous and too relative on the other? To answer this, we must return to a more detailed exploration of the theme of relationality.

3. Relationality and Relativity

A major, if not the major theme running throughout our explorations thus far has been that of relationality. The analysis of reality as dimensional and mediated centered around the symbiotic character of the relationships that interconnect the various aspects and events constituting the real. The examination of knowledge as tacit and embodied interaction highlighted the dynamics of the relationship between the knower and the known in terms of the notion of participation. Our current treatment of the nature and basis of moral responsibility has focused on the relationship between context and mediation. We are now ready to zero-in on the criterion for determining moral value, and here again the notion of relationality comes to the fore.

In light of the ontological and epistemological relevance of relationality, it is hardly surprising that it would suggest itself as the fundamental structure of and criterion for moral judgment as well. If both reality and knowledge come into being and function as basically relational in nature, value would seem to be best characterized in this way too. Moral value, then, is grounded in and must be judged by the essentially relational character of human existence and experience. In short, a given action or pattern of conduct must be said to be good to the degree that it facilitates and enhances the fullness of human relationship; and it must be said to be bad to the degree that it hinders human relationships.

Immediately the question arises as to whether this relational criterion for determining moral value is deontological or teleological in nature. My quick answer is to say "neither," since the shortcomings of both are well known. The former, from Plato to Kant, is in constant danger of pricing virtue out of the market by overstressing its transcendent and absolute character. The latter, from Aristotle to Mill, is equally problematic because it tends to reduce virtue to whatever seems effective and useful at a given time and place. The strengths of each of these traditional approaches to moral value lie precisely where the other's weaknesses arise. Each balances the other, but each excludes the other as well. We need both, yet we cannot have both. The entire history of moral philosophy—including most contemporary formulations—revolves around this dilemma without being able to solve it.

We have, of course, encountered this dilemma before, when considering both being and knowing. The introductory section of this chapter was devoted to pinpointing this same dilemma in ethical theory. In each case, the central issue has centered in the possibility and/or necessity of establishing a transcendent reference point for being, knowing, and doing that can be made meaningful and relevant to common, everyday life. My own proposal has been that we construe transcendence as mediated, rather than as separate and independent, so that it exists and discloses itself *in and through* the more common dimensions of human experience. With respect to moral experience, this would mean focusing on relationality as the primary mediator of a transcendent reference point.

As to whether this approach to morality is essentially deontological or teleological in nature, my initial response was "neither," yet my more considered response is "both." Once again I prefer to slip between the horns of this standard dilemma by proposing a redefinition of the key notion of transcendence. My instinct tells me that no moral judgment can be viable and acceptable that does not in the final analysis serve the most fundamental needs of human existence. Thus I lean toward a teleological interpretation of morality, toward some kind of "deep" utilitarianism. At the same time, however, I must acknowledge that without something like a transcendent reference point, teleological utility seems to implode in on itself for want of a fixed goal at which to aim.

Perhaps the easiest way to clarify the utilitarian's point is to consider a concrete example, one introduced by Kant in his attempt to show the essentially contradictory nature, and thus the immorality, of lying. Kant argues that if someone, armed and serious, comes to your door announcing the intent of killing your spouse and asking if he or she is home, you are morally justified in telling the truth (that your spouse *is* home) since the ensuing murder is the visitor's responsibility. Kant maintains that if you lie and through some fluke the visitor kills your spouse anyway, then you have inserted yourself into the situation and share in the responsibility for the murder. Thus, in Kant's mind, your duty to tell the truth transcends any consideration of the particular advantages and disadvantages of the situation. But most people immediately object to this conclusion, insisting that protecting human life outweighs truth telling, at least in this instance. As W. D. Ross put it, when they conflict, the *good* clearly takes precedence over the *right*.

While it is possible to object to Kant on deontological grounds, arguing that the protection of life is a "higher duty," the same problem arises when one asks for the justification of this duty apart from its value to human life. It surely is inadequate to assume the magic wand of authoritarianism or self-evidentialism and reply, "Well, it just stands on its own!" Nor will it do to invoke the will of God, since either God's will must be interpreted as enhancing human well-being in the deepest sense or it must be seen as arbitrary and dictatorial. The problem is how to combine the relevance of the teleological perspective with the stability of the deontological perspective.

At the abstract level this can be done by realizing that moral standards do not have to be independent of human values in order to be transcendent and stable. Why cannot the values inherent in the moral dimension of experience both *arise* from within this dimension and *emerge* out of the dimensions through which it is mediated? The transcendent quality of moral judgment, like that of cognitive judgment, functions as a "regulative" factor rather than a "substantive" one. It arises from within the process of making moral judgments, as the "universal" at which we all aim, and at the same time it serves to remind us that no particular moral judgment can claim finality. This properly chastened deontological aspect of morality, then, provides its "formal" character, while the teleological aspect provides its "material" character.

Wittgenstein has an exceedingly profound passage in which he points out that the concept of "measurement" and the activity of "measuring" are symbiotic, that it makes no sense to speak of the one as existing apart from the other.[6] Yet, the two poles of this bipolar reality are not reducible to each other, for the standard of measurement—which serves as the criterion in individual acts of measuring—actually grows out of the activity of measuring itself. In the same way, the standards and criteria of morality can be said to emerge out of the actual process of making moral judgments within concrete human contexts. Such standards are truly transcendent in the sense that they serve to focus the goal of and criterion for evaluating the particular actions and judgments out of which they arise. Yet, such standards are not separable from the particulars in relation to which they are endowed with meaning.

Without being willing to endorse every aspect of John Dewey's moral theory, especially his penchant for calling his approach "scientific," I would affirm his overall posture.[7] Far from reducing moral values to matters of mere expediency, as the majority of his critics claim, Dewey sought to ground them in the web of human experience, in order to preserve both their relevance *and* their stability. He sought to rescue moral standards from the abstractions and authoritarianism of traditional philosophy and theology, which render them irrelevant, while at the same time avoiding the pitfalls of subjectivity and absolute relativity. Dewey tried to steer a middle course between these two standard and equally unproductive approaches to moral value.

As a pragmatist (or instrumentalist), Dewey maintained that moral judgments and standards are valuable only if and when they "work." The usual criticism at this point is to ask, "work for whom?," thereby implying that Dewey is guilty of falling into relativism. However, even a cursory reading of Dewey makes it amply clear that his answer to this question would be, "For the greatest number of people, over the longest period of time, in the context which is most appropriate." Granted, it is difficult to determine such factors, and they must be determined by finite and biased human beings; but these considerations do not render such judgments and the viability of a workable consensus impossible. Moreover, even an absolutist in moral theory must engage in interpretation and application, so the human

---

[6]Ludwig Wittgenstein, *Philosophical Investigations* (New York: Macmillan, 1953) #242.

[7]See especially his *Quest for Certainty* (New York: Putnam's Sons, 1960).

factor cannot be eliminated. As a matter of historical and sociopolitical fact, even when moral values have been construed as absolutely transcendent, they have been interpreted and implemented in a wide variety of ways, ways relative to their given setting.

In order to guard against the dogmatism and arrogance that have generally accompanied the understanding of moral values as transcendent, Dewey stressed the usefulness of ethical standards as the final court of appeal. He argued, furthermore, that to pretend our moral judgments are absolute, when in fact they are necessarily finite and subject to change, is to perpetrate far more evil in the world than a flat-out relativism could ever produce. Dewey advocated testing *all* ethical standards and judgments against the common experience of humanity in its effort to sustain itself in community. Such contextual factors as the number of people affected and the span of time involved are highly relevant but the differences among cultures and subcultures must be taken into account as well. Whatever enhances human life in light of these considerations must be judged valuable, right, and good, while whatever is counterproductive to human life is clearly wrong and evil.

> When theories of values do not afford intellectual assistance in framing ideas and beliefs about values that are adequate to direct action, the gap must be filled by other means. If intelligent method is lacking, prejudice, the pressure of immediate circumstance, self-interest and class-interest, traditional customs, institutions of accidental historic origin, are *not* lacking, and they tend to take the place of intelligence. Thus we are led to our main proposition: *Judgments about values are judgments about the conditions and the results of experienced objects; judgments about that which should regulate the formation of our desires, affections and enjoyments.* For whatever decides their formation will determine the main course of our conduct, personal and social.[8]

This way of putting the matter leads directly to the deeper criticism that is often leveled at Dewey's instrumentalism. "Just what," it is asked, "keeps this approach from collapsing into relativism? What will provide the stability that traditional, absolute moral standards provided?" This question focuses once again the assumption that lies behind the modern dilemma of the stalemate between transcendentalism and relativism, namely, that an absolute reference point for moral values and stability in moral judgments *necessarily* go together. Dewey challenged this assump-

---

[8]Ibid., 265; my italics.

tion by contending that an experiential grounding for moral values does not exclude moral stability. In this regard I concur fully with Dewey.

In the final analysis, every deontological interpretation of morality—including that of Plato, Kant, and Alasdair MacIntyre—that does not result in purely arbitrary, unreasonable tyranny must justify its standards on the basis of an appeal to their effectiveness in human experience. What could it possibly mean to say that a given standard of conduct is morally right, even though it leads to human misery? For that matter, what could it mean to contend that while such a standard must coincide with human well-being, its justification is not based therein? What other grounding could there be, short of vicious circularity or blind fiat? Thoughtful and sincere consideration of which forms of behavior are most conducive to human life provides sufficient stability to render moral judgments functional.

The above move constitutes a redefinition of transcendence with respect to the grounding of moral value. Whatever values establish themselves in the give-and-take of human existence throughout time and across cultures (giving ample consideration to the relativities necessitated by cultural differences) can thereby be termed "transcendent." Such transcendence arises *within* the patterns and processes of that dimension to which it pertains and is mediated in and through the other dimensions of experience. It goes "beyond" the sum of the particulars constituting the mediating dimensions without existing independently of them. *Mediated transcendence*, therefore, as a regulative, formal criterion provides the reference point necessary for grounding moral values, without requiring the price of dogmatism or irrelevancy entailed by the traditional notion of transcendence.

Before concluding this section, let me place its central concern within the framework of biblical ethics, so as to give it some concrete exemplification. Frequently the Ten Commandments (Exodus 20) are thought of as transcendent in the absolutist sense, since they are said to express the will of God for humankind. It is clear, however, from reflection on the specifics of these commandments, as well as on the circumstances under which they were stated, that they were designed to enhance the well-being of those to whom they were given as well as humanity at large. For the most part, God is not represented in the Old Testament as one who simply establishes commandments willy-nilly or as a being primarily concerned about divine well-being. Such a being would be nothing more than a despot, unworthy of worship or obedience. Rather, the God of the Hebrews is on the whole portrayed as one who desires meaningful and enriching relationship with and among human persons. The Ten

Commandments were given as a means of expressing one's commitment to live in harmony with God's desires, not as a means of earning God's favor.

Moving on to the New Testament, the ethical teachings of Jesus were clearly aimed at helping people live as members of God's family, as God's creation, and as brothers and sisters. Not only did Jesus offer fresh interpretations of Mosaic law ("You have heard it said, . . . but I say to you" Matt. 5:21-48) and challenge the legalism of his day ("Beware of the leaven of the Pharisees," Matt. 16:6), but he refused to carry out the dictates of the law whenever it conflicted with the well-being of the persons involved ("Nor do I condemn you," John 8). The justification given for this general posture on Jesus' part was not some transcendental Form, or the law of noncontradiction, or even a new revelation from God. Rather, it was that "the lame walk, the blind are given sight, the captives are liberated" (Luke 7:22). As Jesus said in a different but related context, "By their fruits you shall know them" (Matt. 7:16).

The humanitarian grounding for moral values in the teachings of Jesus is focused pointedly and irrevocably in his reply to those who complained that in doing good on the Sabbath he and his followers were breaking the law. Jesus said, "The Sabbath was made for human beings, human beings were not made for the Sabbath" (Mark 2:27). The full significance of this statement must be allowed to sink in. He was speaking here of one of the Ten Commandments, not one of the arbitrary laws of the Pharisees. After all of the necessary qualifiers have been inserted, the fact remains that in Jesus' mind human well-being is the final grounding for moral value.

Finally consider the ethical teachings of Paul. Although there are occasional passages that seem to indicate otherwise, the central thrust of Paul's moral concern was directed against the legalism of those who sought to interpret the Gospel within the confines of Mosaic law. The essential quality of this rejection of legalism is powerfully focused in the letter to the Galatians, which stresses the moral freedom of the person who follows Christ. Elsewhere, Paul sums up his general posture by reminding his readers that while the letter of the law brings death, the spirit of the law "gives life" (2 Cor. 3:6). Here again, the quality of human relationship is employed as the criterion for moral judgment. This criterion is both relevant and relative, while at the same time transcending any particular individual or cultural point of view.

4. Dialogue and Persuasion

The preceding section argued that to ground moral values in the deepest and broadest needs and capacities of our common humanity is to provide a basis that is at once *relevant to* and *transcendent of* each and every specific manifestation thereof. Thus, morality can be both relational and contextual, while remaining transcendent in the mediational sense. It still remains the case, however, that particular moral judgments must be clarified and justified by means of the dialectical dynamics of human reason and discussion. No universal agreement can be promised, only common commitment to the process of pursuing such universal agreement. This "universal intent," balanced by participation in the "community of explorers," is a sufficient basis for confidence in our moral activity. It still remains to be discussed just what the concrete dynamics of our common search for effective and lasting moral values are.

In our search for a common context for moral value, we will have recourse to *dialogue* and *persuasion*. A dialogical posture is different from either a parochial posture or an adversarial posture. Both of these more standard approaches to the question of differences about moral foundations undercut mutuality and growth, the former through irrelevance and arrogance, the latter through hostility and coercion. Alfred North Whitehead said that the fundamental insight of the Christian religion is its discernment that God's will is accomplished through persuasion rather than coercion. If this be true, and I believe that it is, then any Christian approach to moral differences must be so characterized as well. Unfortunately, this has not been the case throughout much, if not most, of the Christian era, but there are signs that things are changing. Such change is mandatory in an increasingly pluralistic culture such as our own.

A helpful way of thinking about these different approaches has been suggested by James McClendon and James Smith in their book *Understanding Religious Convictions*.[9] In the context of discussing the question of the truth of religious beliefs, they analyze three major possible postures. At one extreme stand those who argue that even though different people have different points of view about what the truth is, there is only one view that is correct. McClendon and Smith call this posture "Non-perspectivism." At the other extreme stand those who insist that truth is strictly a function of a given theoretical framework of specific cultural

---

[9](Notre Dame: Notre Dame University Press, 1975).

context. This radically relativistic posture they designate as "Hard-per-spectivism." In between these extremes they locate and recommend a posture that, while acknowledging the importance of cultural and theo-retic context in determining truth, also affirms both the possibility and the advisability of searching for common commitments and assumptions across these different contexts. They call this posture "Soft-perspectiv-ism" and characterize it as an approach that seeks both to promote mu-tual understanding and to explore the possibility of eventual—if only partial—agreement in a pluralistic context.

> If I believe in God (am convinced of God) in a pluralistic world, a world in which I know there are men of good will who do not so believe, then my faith, if justified at all, must be a faith which takes account of that very plu-ralism which in part denies my faith. It must be faith justifiable (I must be justified by my faith?) in a world which includes unfaith. Conversely, if I disbelieve, believe in no God, am convinced no God exists, in a world in which I know there are men who do so believe, then my conviction, if jus-tified at all, must be one which takes account of that fact—it must be athe-ism in a world which includes faith. The pluralism which we envisage, then, does not obviate justification nor require narrowness of outlook, but it does require that the pluralism itself shall be internalized, so that it becomes a factor which my convictions take into account.[10]

I would recommend the implementation of this Soft-perspectivism in order to resolve differences concerning the basis of moral value. It not only provides a rationale for continued dialogue about and increased mutual understanding of these differences, but it also holds open the possibility that at deeper levels such differences can be overcome, both through ne-gotiation and perhaps through the discovery of more basic commonali-ties. Such a posture, clearly, calls for a combination of confidence and humility. Those who participate in cross-perspectival explorations must value both their own commitments and those of others, while remaining open to modification and fresh insight. Dialogue entails both honesty and listening, and persuasion requires both respect and commitment to the value of agreement.

I am committed to the posture of Soft-perspectivism, partly because it leaves the door open to further discussion but mostly because I believe that since all people share a common humanity and environment, their

---

[10]Ibid., 183.

basic values will be essentially similar. The embodied and linguistic character of our existence, together with the commonality of our need to understand one another in order to maintain and enhance that existence, all serve to justify a commitment to the search for a universal grounding of moral values. Although I am not prepared here to offer a definition of such a grounding, it would seem evident that mutual respect for the life and worth of all people and cultures, as well as an affirmation of the necessity for dialogue and cooperation, would be fundamental to it.

There remains, to be sure, the difficulty of what to do about the fact that at any given time certain individuals, groups, and nations behave in such a manner as to threaten these basic values. While the commitment to tolerance and dialogue entails a flexible and conciliatory posture with respect to such behavior, it does not require unilateral acceptance. A perspective that essentially denies the rights of other perspectives cannot itself be tolerated, lest the entire fabric of mutuality and dialogue be destroyed. The practical decisions involved in determining exactly when and where this basic level of tolerance has been violated are extremely difficult and can only be worked out in the give-and-take of my day-by-day personal and social political activity. Needless to say, there is a pressing need for an increased commitment to tolerance, as well as to creative and effective ways of dealing with its denial, on the part of all people in today's world.

Not only is a dialogical and contextual posture with regard to the question of moral value the only viable approach to the *possibility* of achieving a common basis, but it will in fact prove to be the means for achieving its *actuality* as well. For, by means of increased dialogical interaction at the level of ethical decision and behavior, we can create a dynamic and a context that will mediate the enriching and encompassing character of a transcendent moral dimension in which such activity can be grounded universally.

The theological basis for this belief is the conviction that we all are created in the image of God and that this image provides both the framework and the patterns by means of which such moral transcendence can be known. It is, however, not necessary for those participating in the task of discerning this transcendence to be aware of or acknowledge a theological perspective. Such activity can and will be carried on in and of itself, in much the same way as the principles governing our physical environment are operative whether or not we understand physics and chemistry. While religious belief is not required for the development and enactment of a viable morality, neither are the two mutually exclusive.

Thus, it is both possible and desirable for those of different persuasions at this level to work together at the level of moral value, both conceptually and practically.

A concrete example can be helpful here of how a dialogical approach to the resolution of a basic difference in moral perspectives might look. I shall offer the case of radically opposed views on the morality of abortion as an instance where the application of Soft-perspectivism might prove extremely helpful. The idea here is not to pretend to arrive at a final solution of this highly complex and important issue, but simply to illustrate how progress can be made when those who disagree strongly are mutually committed to the process of honest exploration and understanding, with an eye to reaching a common perspective.

At the extreme poles of the continuum on the abortion issue stand those who are opposed to it for *any* reason (commonly called the pro-life position) and those who feel it should be exclusively a decision for each pregnant woman herself (commonly called the pro-choice position). Now if these people were prepared to enter into honest dialogue aimed at resolution, something like the following scenario could develop. The pro-choice people might be willing to admit that the vast majority of abortions in America are obtained by white upper-middle-class women who are clearly in a position to have and care for a child, both physically and financially. For far too many women, having an abortion is more a matter of convenience than need. The pro-life people, for their part, might well admit that in some extreme cases an abortion may be justified. Cases of rape, incest, and severe medical complications would seem to qualify in this regard.

In addition to this concession, those on the "right" of the continuum, the pro-life forces, might move toward the middle by acknowledging that a substantial decrease in the number of abortions will necessitate a dramatic increase in the need for social services for the mothers and children involved. Pre-marital counseling, health facilities, and financial support suggest themselves immediately as services that local and federal governments ought to supply. In addition, thorough sex education, especially concerning the use of contraceptives, ought to be more widely available. On the "left" side of the continuum, the pro-choice supporters should be prepared to admit that there are viable alternatives to abortion that women seeking abortion ought to consider. So frequently, the possibility of having a baby and making it available for adoption through a reliable agency never even occurs to those who have abortions. This alternative seems to be an equitable compromise in relation to the responsibilities entailed by becoming pregnant.

Those who are pro-choice could also move closer to the center of the continuum by affirming the need for our culture to strengthen the webbing that undergirds family relationships and interpersonal commitment. There is, unfortunately, a great deal of individualism fueling pro-choice advocacy. Although it definitely is necessary to liberate women from the oppression of traditional views of their "place" and worth, it is equally important not to replace a patriarchical hierarchy with an atomism that causes the fabric of society to disintegrate. This move toward the center might well be matched by getting those of the pro-life persuasion to examine the sociopolitical causes that have given rise to the current crisis over the abortion issue. In particular, the double standard that pervades our society with respect to male and female sexual activity and responsibility needs to be thoroughly dismantled. Also, the importance in a pluralistic society of distinguishing between *endorsing* one's own moral and/or religious values and *imposing* them on others needs to be stressed.

The forgoing concessions on the part of both sides might lead to a compromise with respect to the current laws concerning abortion. Although there are always risks and abuses involved in such policies, the possibility of setting up a committee (composed of the pregnant woman, her doctor, a social worker, the father, and perhaps a minister and/or a lawyer) suggests itself as a viable means of deciding what is the most ethical course of action. Both sides in the present debate would have to agree that morality is a *corporate* responsibility. It cannot be imposed by some individuals on others, even if they constitute the majority, nor is it the function of a totally private decision-making process. On the other hand, while morality cannot be legislated, laws can serve to keep people from exploiting one another on the basis of their individual biases.

What might well be the central issue in this important and difficult discussion is the question of when human life actually begins. Pro-life supporters generally argue that it begins at conception, while some pro-choice advocates contend that it begins when a child participates in human social relations. The real difficulty here, as in most questions of moral choice, is that life is a *process* that does not easily divide up into clear-cut segments or submit to convenient designations. In other words, "human life" does not come on the scene already labeled as such; it is human beings themselves who must decide when and how to apply the terms they use in relation to the world in which they live. Moreover, as is often the case, there simply is no single criterion by which to make these decisions. In practice, they must be made on the basis of a cluster of variable criteria. Thus, there is a pressing need for dialogue on such issues, since they cannot be settled solely on the basis of custom, belief, law, or even empirical data.

One difficulty with saying that human life begins at conception is that this way of speaking ignores the obvious preparatory character of the prenatal process. To say that a tiny embryo *is* human, rather than *potentially* human, is to overlook the vast differences between embryonic and human existence. Another difficulty is that this view raises problems with respect to such issues as the legal rights and obligations of fetuses. On the other side, it must also be admitted that to define human life strictly in terms of participation in social relations raises very serious problems with respect to the justifiability of infanticide. It would seem, then, that both sides in this discussion must move toward a more central position, one that seeks a more viable notion of when human life begins.

Some pro-lifers have been willing to accept the possibility of marking the beginning of human life at the inception of certain processes such as brain waves and/or heart beat, or at the appearance of human features in the fetus, or simply on the basis of three- or six-month time intervals. In this latter connection, many pro-choice supporters have conceded that abortion is not justifiable after a certain stage of development has been reached: six months is often used as a marker, or whenever the fetus can be judged to have the ability to survive premature birth. Clearly, concessions such as these are helpful in reaching a workable resolution on the abortion issue, and they are compatible with the possibility of a corporate or committee decision as well.

In my own view, a strong case can be made for following the conventional and transcultural practice of defining human life in terms of birth itself. Not only is this the point at which names are traditionally given—which is an exceedingly crucial factor both psychologically and sociologically—but it is at birth that a fetus actually comes into the world as a being separate from its mother. More pointedly, it is at birth when the vital processes of independent breathing and nourishment commence. Such a view does not, however, completely justify abortion, since it is consistent with denying the abortion of any fetus that could survive premature birth. This view is also consistent with the exploration of other alternatives, such as adoption, by means of a well-chosen and responsible advisory committee.

All the above factors and considerations not only point to the necessity and possibility of working toward a compromise view on the abortion issue, but they illustrate the mediational character of a contextual approach to the grounding of moral values as well. A transcendent grounding can be achieved through dialogue and persuasion, although admittedly it will involve a fresh notion of transcendence. Only by means of such a redefinition can the standoff between traditional absolutism and modern relativism be overcome. By focusing on relationality and contextuality, the viability of reaching a helpful and stable basis for moral values through open and open-ended dialogue is greatly increased. This ongoing process is both necessary and adequate for the mediation of realistically transcendent values.

Five

SAYING:

Meaning

as Active and Creative

Linguisticality is, along with embodiment, one of the primary dimensions of the human way of being in the world. Moreover, it is by means of language that we bring together and express the dimensional and mediated character of being, the interactive and tacit nature of knowledge, as well as the relational and contextual quality of moral activity.

1. Words and Persons

The dominant view of the nature of linguistic communication among modern thinkers has been that of the "picture theory of meaning." According to this view of linguistic activity, words function as names or labels for the various things and relations that make up our world. The word *cat*, for example, refers to or names that small, furry, domesticated feline animal in the corner; the word *mat*, in turn, is the label for the piece of carpet upon which the cat is sitting, while the words *is* and *on* represent the relation of the cat to the mat. Thus, when those words are strung together they form a proposition, "The cat is on the mat," which seeks to picture the state of affairs in the corner. Such a view of language serves to limit the central purpose of linguistic activity to the process of transferring information about the world.

The locus classicus of this view of language is, of course, the young Wittgenstein's *Tractatus Logico-Philosophicus.*[1] The ontology that is entailed thereby was worked out quite thoroughly by Bertrand Russell in his "Lectures on Logical Atomism."[2] The main result of this view of the relation between language and reality is the division of the world into isolatable "facts," which are related to each other only externally and stand in one-to-one correspondence to the sum total of true propositions that constitute human knowledge. These "atomic facts" are said to be knowable through—and only through—sensory observation and/or inductive inference, thereby eliminating the possibility of transcendence at the outset. This general approach, which is aptly termed "logical empiricism" and represents a synthesis of the work of Hume and Kant, is the epitome of modern, English-speaking philosophy well into the middle of the twentieth century.

The correlative results from the philosophy of language, according to the above point of view, is that only those statements that can be construed as picturing states of affairs, in addition to those which are the function of strictly logical discourse, can be said to be *cognitively meaningful.* For, only these statements are subject to verification through sensory observation. All other linguistic activity is said to be noncognitive in character, serving only to express emotions, give commands, ask questions, and so on. Thus, once again, any attempt to speak about that which might transcend the empirical dimension of human experience was eliminated at the outset. A. J. Ayer's *Language, Truth and Logic* still represents the most influential presentation of this overall approach.[3]

Despite the many caveats and modifications that continued criticism of logical empiricism and its "verifiability criterion of meaning" have forced, it is surprising how much of contemporary philosophy still maintains an unspoken dependence on this general point of view. What is generally overlooked in all the controversy over the basis of linguistic meaning is the simple fact that language is, after all, a human activity. It is persons who speak and therefore persons, not statements, who *mean.* In other words, to focus on the meaningfulness or meaninglessness of individual statements is to obscure the fact that it is persons speaking to each

---

[1](New York: Humanities Press, 1961).

[2]*Monist* 28 (1918): 495-527.

[3](New York: Dover, 1946.)

other that constitutes the fundamental matrix of meaning. Thus meaning is in reality a function of the *use* to which people put language in the context of shared tasks and community.

It was the mature Wittgenstein who made it abundantly clear that speech is a social activity. He suggested thinking of language as a tool by means of which persons accomplish things in their common world and existence. Just as we need a variety of tools in order to carry out the various tasks of building and maintenance, so there are a variety of uses to which language can and must be put. The meaning of any given utterance, then, can only be determined by knowing who said it, to whom, where, when, how, and why. Transferring information is, after all, only one of those things we do by means of speech. Moreover, people do not even do this for its own sake, but only in a specific context and for a concrete purpose. We say "The cat is on the mat" in order to reassure a child, for instance, or to get someone to remove the cat, or to provide an example in a philosophical discussion, and so on.

In addition, Wittgenstein called our attention to the fact that our linguistic activity tends to develop into and follow specific patterns and processes, which he termed "language-games." Wittgenstein's use of the metaphors of tools and games in no way implied an arbitrariness or triviality about linguistic activity. Rather, they were meant to indicate language's *pragmatic* and *relational* character in contrast to the traditional emphasis on its representational function. At the heart of speech lie the tasks and interactions of everyday life, and in and around these tasks specific conventions and connections develop that constitute the context within which verbal behavior takes on meaning.

Review the multiplicity of language-games in the following examples:

Giving orders and obeying them—
Describing the appearance of an object or giving its measurements—
Constructing an object from a description (a drawing)—
Reporting an event—
Speculating about an event—
Forming and testing a hypothesis—
Presenting the results of an experiment in tables and diagrams—
Making up a story and reading it—
Play-acting—
Singing catches—
Guessing riddles—
Making a joke, telling it—
Solving a problem in practical arithmetic—

Translating from one language into another—
Asking, thanking, cursing, greeting, praying.[4]

Thus we weave various language-games or conventional patterns that serve as the bearers of significance in and around our shared tasks and activities. These patterns, along with the specifics of use and context, *mediate* the meaning of the locutions we utter. It is both interesting and instructive to note that small children begin to participate in the various moves of these language-games prior to acquiring specific vocabulary. They generally become familiar with and practice (on a play telephone, perhaps) the intonations that indicate such activities as giving instructions, orders, and questions, telling jokes, and the like without using actual words. Moreover, we all learn to tell the difference between saying "The door is open" as a description, as an imperative ("Close the door"), as an invitation ("Drop by anytime"), or as an encouragement ("Go for it"). There are certain patterns of reciprocation that enable our linguistic activity to bear meaning.

It should be perfectly clear from the above considerations and examples not only that the representation of states of affairs is far from the only purpose of speech, but that it is essentially parasitic on broader, more complex patterns of significance. People do not speak primarily to convey information; rather, they convey information in order to accomplish a wide variety of tasks, and they do so by means of established yet flexible patterns of linguistic and nonlinguistic behavior. Mirroring the world is only one function of speech, and it gets its significance from the fact that linguistic activity in general is a social and ongoing enterprise. It is persons who speak, and thus it is persons who mean. Apart from the concrete tasks and social interaction of everyday life, the "propositions" so emphasized in modern philosophy are a fifth wheel, signifying nothing.

At an even deeper level, Wittgenstein sought to ground linguistic activity, as a pragmatic and social phenomenon, in the very nature of the human way of being in the world, in what he called the "human form of life." In my view, what he had in mind here was the fact that linguisticality is an inherent and essential dimension of what it means to be human and that speaking is inextricably bound up with the other crucial aspects of human existence, such as physicality and sociality. It is through our linguistic activity that we integrate our interaction with physical and

---

[4]*Philosophical Investigations* (New York: Macmillan, 1953) #23.

social reality; thus language *mediates* and largely *constitutes* our world. In like manner, it is by means of speech that we come to think as well as express our thoughts. Language is neither optional nor ancillary to thought and reality: it is integral and essential to our participating in them, qua humans, at all. Just as our use of speech, and thus meaning itself, is grounded in specific contexts and social patterns, so these contexts and language-games are themselves grounded in the needs, capacities, and aspirations marking the human way of life.

All of this is clearly and powerfully evident in the life of Helen Keller, who stated that prior to becoming a participant in linguistic activity she was a mere "phantom," unable to engage in "intentional" behavior and so merely responding randomly to various external and internal stimuli.[5] It was by means of speech—in her case, tactile sign language—that she became a human, capable of making and keeping (or breaking) promises, following instructions, telling jokes, grasping abstract concepts, creating stories, and so on. It is the same with so-called feral children who spend their formative years with various animals. Their basic way of being in the world is largely a nonhuman form of life, and under stress they generally drop what little human sociality and linguisticality they later acquire, reverting to animal behavior such as howling and moving about on all fours.

Not only does this Wittgensteinian way of understanding language render the picture theory of meaning and logical atomism obsolete by revealing the incredible complexity and depth of linguistic activity, it opens up a way of construing language as capable of expressing transcendence as well.

The underlying assumptions of both the picture theory of meaning and logical atomism entail a commitment to the value and possibility of *absolute precision* and *explicit articulation* in linguistic expression. That is, the assumption of a one-to-one correlation between words and various aspects of the world makes it both possible and preferable to spell out each and every quality and relationship pertaining to any given object or state of affairs. This way of thinking about meaningful linguistic activity entails the exclusion of any mode of speech that is not susceptible to such one-dimensional analysis. Thus, from the outset all talk of the transcendent is eliminated from the sphere of meaningful discourse.

---

[5]*Teacher* (Garden City: Doubleday, 1955) 75.

Some thinkers—such as Paul Tillich, for example—have sought to overcome this positivist approach by totally severing the significance of language about the transcendent from all forms of empirical discourse.[6] To my mind, this sort of "divide and conquer" maneuver only serves to legitimize yet another version of positivism, that of *symbolic* expression. The dichotomy between literal and symbolic language is no more helpful than was that between cognitive and noncognitive speech. Once again, as with Platonic and related dualisms, the transcendent is thereby relegated to a realm that lies beyond the social and everyday dimensions of human experience. This move renders all expressions of the transcendent as irrelevant as they are unverifiable.

An emphasis on the social character of linguistic meaning, however, serves to lead us beyond both the flatness of positivism and the "word-salad" of symbolism. In focusing on the mediation of meaning in and through the participation of the speaker in the give-and-take of linguistic activity, this emphasis both exemplifies and substantiates how significance transcends mere signification without being separable from it. Mediated meaning is at once transcendent of and dependent on that by which it is mediated, because it is embodied in the latter without being exhausted by it. The notions of "use in context," "language-games," and "forms of life" each serve to demonstrate that this is the case.

As noted, the meaning of a particular utterance will vary in any given context, depending on by whom, where, when, how, to whom, and why it is uttered. Such nuances can never, and need never, be fully articulated for communication to take place; full articulation and precision are replaced as ideals by *adequate* articulation and *significant* precision. Nevertheless, there can be no communication whatsoever apart from the particulars comprising the specific context of a given utterance. The meaning comes in and through such particulars without being reducible to them. Therefore, the fundamental structure of linguistic communication is itself an example of the reality of mediated transcendence.

The examples introduced earlier on—namely, "The cat is on the mat" and "The door is open"—are clearly cases wherein the meaning is grounded in the context but is at the same time never exhausted by any specific account of the contextual particulars. In like manner, to speak of the divine in terms of strength, wisdom, love, and friendship in the human context displays this same mediational pattern whereby the tran-

---

[6]*Dynamics of Faith* (New York: Harper & Row, 1956) xx.

scendent dimension is communicated in and through the natural dimension. Here, too, one must look to the particulars of the context in order to discern that which is claimed to transcend them. Ian Ramsey's well-known "model-qualifier" pattern helpfully pinpoints this notion of mediated transcendence in linguistic activity.

> Metaphors then are not just link devices between different contexts. They are necessarily grounded in inspiration.
> Generalizing, we say that metaphorical expressions occur when two situations strike us in such a way as to reveal what includes them but is no mere combination of them both. Metaphors and models, both enabling us to be articulate about an insight, are thus the basic currency for mystery, and we can spend our lives elucidating ever more faithfully the mystery in which metaphors and models are born.[7]

This same dynamic operates at the level of language-games and forms of life. The social character of linguistic activity is especially prominent at these levels, and once again the meaning of a given utterance can be seen as mediated in and through the patterns constituting it. This is particularly true with respect to the significance of talk of the transcendent, since it is extremely difficult—if not impossible—to discern the meaning of such utterances apart from a thorough understanding of the *community* within which they function. This observation does not constitute an appeal to some mysterious special knowledge or linguistic fideism. To be sure, the language-games in which we participate criss-cross and overlap in a wide variety of nonexclusivist ways. Nevertheless, to proceed as if linguistic meaning can be abstracted from its pragmatic and social contexts is to betray an exceedingly shallow understanding of the nature of linguistic activity.

2. Words and Deeds

In addition to linguistic meaning being anchored in the social activity of speaking persons, it is also inextricably connected with the things such speakers accomplish in the world. Thus, the relationship between language and reality, not unlike that between language and thought, is far more complex and dynamic than most philosophers have acknowledged. Far from there being a merely static, one-to-one correlation be-

---

[7]*Models and Mystery* (New York: Oxford University Press, 1963) 53.

tween language and thought on the one hand, and between language and the world on the other hand, these relationships can be seen to be quite reciprocal and functional in nature. In this section we shall explore briefly this interactive dynamic between language, thought, and reality.

According to the picture theory of meaning, language *represents* both inner thoughts and the outer world. The general idea is that first we think things or encounter things (or think about things we have previously encountered, but which are not now present) and then we speak about them to others. Through language we are said to communicate our thoughts and/or to signify various objects and aspects of the world. Let us consider each side of this twofold representationalist view of linguistic meaning.

Although we sometimes do struggle to match up our words with our thoughts, such matching is hardly the norm in the relation between words and thoughts. To begin with, it is clear that we do not acquire language by first having thoughts and then learning the appropriate words for them. Rather, it is by gradually coming to participate in language that we develop what we call "thoughts" in the first place. Moreover, when we talk as active members of a speaking community, our thoughts and our words are two sides of the same coin; or better, we think in and through our words, not independently of them. As a case in point, I have begun this very sentence without any prior knowledge of which words I shall use along the way. We speak and our words *mediate* our thoughts; they do not *represent* them.

Human communication is not dependent upon there being a one-to-one correlation between the thoughts in the speaker's mind and those in the hearers', if by 'thoughts' we mean mental images and the like. When you say "salt" at the breakfast table, I may actually picture Lot's wife and you may be reminded of the disarmament talks, but communication has taken place if you get the salt passed to you—and it has not if you do not. Conversely, even if we both think of Utah, we have not communicated— and thus have not *meant* the same thing—if your request "misfires," to use J. L. Austin's term. Linguistic meaning is a function of whether or not certain tasks and/or deeds are accomplished.

On the other side of the coin, consider the fact that often we actually *alter* the world about which we speak in the act of speaking. It was J. L. Austin who first called this "performative" character of language to the attention of the philosophical world. He pointed out that in a sincere act of saying the words "I apologize," we actually perform the deed of apologizing. Austin made it clear that this performative quality of speech pervades a great deal of language and thus undercuts the notion that the primary, if not exclusive, function of language is to represent reality. In performative utterances our speech functions as a part of reality by altering it.

As he examined this active character of language more closely, Austin found that his original distinction between performatives and what he called "constatives" (descriptives) foundered on the fact that even propositional descriptions have a performative quality to them: even "The cat is on the mat" is implicitly prefaced with the phrase "I state that . . . ," and stating is itself an act that is performed by the speaker. As we discovered in the previous section, statements are made by persons and cannot exist in a cognitive vacuum. Thus, all speech constitutes a contribution to reality, since deeds and events are every bit as real as objects and qualities.

In his last extensive work, *How to Do Things with Words*, Austin sought to revise and revitalize his original insight. He suggested that we think of each "speech-act" as composed of three main dimensions or forces: (1) the *locutionary*, consisting of the simple uttering of certain words, with their conventional yet frequently ambiguous meanings and syntax; (2) the *illocutionary*, constituting the purpose for which the utterance was made, such as to inform, warn, encourage, entertain; and (3) the *perlocutionary*, namely the response of the hearer(s) resulting from the utterance, what Austin termed the "uptake." His fundamental concern was to establish that no analysis of the meaning of a given utterance is complete until each of these aspects of the speech-act has been considered.

> We first distinguished a group of things we do in saying something, which together we summed up by saying we perform a *locutionary act,* which is roughly equivalent to uttering a certain sentence with a certain sense and reference, which again is roughly equivalent to 'meaning' in the traditional sense. Second, we said that we also perform *illocutionary acts* such as informing, ordering, warning, undertaking, &c., i.e. utterances which have a certain (conventional) force. Thirdly, we may also perform *perlocutionary acts:* what we bring about or achieve *by* saying something, such as convincing, persuading, deterring, and even, say, surprising or misleading. Here we have three, if not more, different senses or *dimensions* of the "use of a sentence" or of "the use of language."[8]

---

[8]*How to Do Things with Words* (Cambridge: Harvard University Press, 1962) 108.

Unfortunately, the vast majority of those who have made use of Austin's analysis have fallen into the very atomism his holistic account sought to avoid. For, they have begun by dividing these dimensions or forces into separate acts and have focused on what they call the "propositional speech-act" as the most significant philosophically.[9] Although they fly the colors of the post-Wittgensteinian commitments, such thinkers betray their inherent positivism when they *isolate* what Austin sought to *integrate*, when they revert to the fact/value and true/false dichotomies that Austin sought to push beyond. The clear implications of Austin's most mature work are that the relationship between language and the world is far more integral and reciprocal than traditional philosophers, even when disguised in contemporary idioms, will allow.

In fact, the three dimensions of any given speech-act are essentially symbiotic in character, for each presupposes and gives rise to the other. Locutions (1) would never arise, let alone be used (2), if people did not have things they wished to accomplish with other people (3). At the same time, the idea of getting things done through language (3) would never come up if there were no conventional utterances (1) to use for such purposes (2). It appears that language simply arrived on the scene full-blown, since each of its dimensions is dependent on the others. As a matter of fact, there is no reason to believe that language has evolved from less complex to more complex levels, since even the most primal peoples have highly sophisticated languages.

The overall point here is that language is an integral part of reality itself, rather than being an ancillary and optional appendage of it. Language is inextricably tied to the world in which we live by virtue of being, along with embodiment, our most fundamental way of interacting with and altering that world. Linguistic deeds and events are vital features of reality, as substantial and significant as chairs, jumps, persons, and ideas.

Let us consider each of these aspects of linguistic activity in turn and then describe its bearing on the question of transcendence. The focus is, once again, on the notion of mediation, both in terms of what is *said* and in terms of what is *intended* in a given utterance.

First, it should be clear that the meaning of what is said is mediated in and through the vocabulary and grammatical features constituting the locutionary dimension of speech. Thus, although it is impossible for linguistic meaning to be communicated apart from some specific conven-

---

[9]Cf. John Searle, *Speech Acts* (Cambridge: at the University Press, 1970).

tional signs and patterns, the meaning mediated by these conventions cannot be reduced to or limited by them. If the meaning were equatable with such conventions, then no possibility would exist for ambiguity and creativity. Clearly, any given utterance must be capable of bearing meanings that go beyond the mere "letter" of vocabulary and grammar in order for language to function and grow.

If ambiguity were eliminated, language would (1) require an astronomical number of words and rules to accommodate all of the things people wish to say and do through speech, and (2) be impossible for a child to acquire, since each utterance would be absolutely "context-specific," yielding no generalizations or transfer learning. In effect, each word would be a proper name and would have to be introduced afresh on each occasion.

Not only would the elimination of ambiguity from language be impractical, but it frequently would be counterproductive as well. Very often we deliberately speak in ways that leave the parameters of our meaning at least somewhat open-ended. Diplomacy, whether personal or political, often calls for a mode of speech that seeks the lowest common denominator in order to facilitate initial agreement and further discussion. After all, we must begin talking in general terms before we can speak more specifically, and even the definitions guiding specific linguistic use must be given in other, more general terms.

Then, too, the creative use of language trades on the open-textured character of speech. Metaphor, parable, paradox, and irony, for example, all depend on the polysignificant nature of linguistic activity. It is the open-ended, double-meaning quality of language that enables us to describe, express, and even discern some of the deepest and most peculiar aspects of experienced reality. Such meaning is clearly mediated in and through the interaction between definitions, conventions, context, intent, results, and so on. Thus, linguistic meaning is essentially indirect, since it can never lie simply on the "surface," but needs to be grasped through interaction with others and the world.

This same mediational dynamic comes into play when we focus on understanding the intentionality embodied in other people's verbal and nonverbal behavior. What a person says and does, strictly on the physical level of speaking and doing, is the medium of his intentions without his being reducible to or equatable with such actions. Even though intentions can only be known in and through behavior, it does not follow that intentions are nothing other than behavior. On the other hand, the sense in which intentions transcend behavior is mediational in nature, since they cannot be isolated from it, yet no account of behavior can exhaust and/or specify them precisely. Just when we think we might be able to establish a one-to-one correspondence between a particular statement or deed on the one hand and a specific intention or meaning on the other, an alternative possibility suggests itself.

To be sure, this does not mean that it is impossible to know what another person's intentions are by means of what that person says and does. The open-textured character of speech and behavior must not be confused with absolute fluidity. This seems to me to be the mistake made by extreme deconstructionists. Our linguistic and behavioral conventions do establish the parameters out of which the higher level of meaning emerges. These conventions are always necessary to, but never sufficient for, meaning and intention.

It is this notion of mediation, once again, that opens the way to the recovery of transcendence. The relationship between persons and deeds, as well as that between persons and words, reveals a pattern in which *intangible* reality—such as meaning and intentionality—exists and is known in and through *tangible* reality without being separable from it or equatable with it. Thinking of divine transcendence as structured by this mediational pattern provides a way of going beyond the traditional stand-off between dualists and naturalists. The transcendent dimension, the divine, is present in and known through the other dimensions of human experience without being independent of or reducible to them. Analogously, what persons mean or intend is mediated in and through their verbal and nonverbal behavior, through their words and deeds.

This revised view of transcendence as mediated does not do away with the mysterious and intractable character of the divine, since that which is mediated can never be encompassed by that through which it is mediated. Thinking of transcendence in this way simply serves to remind us that it makes no sense to speak of the divine existing and acting *beyond* our possible experience and knowledge; this way of speaking itself can only be generated and have meaning *within* the dimensions of human experience and knowledge. Because these dimensions are flexible and open-ended, there will always be fresh aspects of transcendence to discover and explore.

This view of transcendence as mediated does not allow for the reduction of the divine to the natural; instead, it affirms the reality of a richer, more comprehensive dimension. On the other hand, the notion of mediated transcendence does entail the anchoring of the intangible in the tangible, the grounding of the divine in the natural, in the same way as meaning and intentions are rooted in speech and action without being exhaustively explained thereby. Intangible realities are *qualitative* in nature; and though they must necessarily be encountered within the matrix of meaning structured by *quantitative,* tangible human contexts and interactions, they are at the same time ultimately more than these contexts and interactions.

3. Words and Worlds

In addition to the forgoing features of linguistic activity, there is also what might be called its "Orphic" character. By this, I mean its ability to construct and constitute the reality within which we live. Just as Orpheus was said to be able to call the world forth by his singing, so we can be said to call our world or worlds into being by speaking. There are at least three levels of human experience in which this Orphic character functions.

To begin with, there is the common, everyday sense in which we shape our experience and that of others by means of the particular words we choose in a given situation. If we call a person a "wimp," a "chick," or a "nigger," we actually contribute to the creation of such realities. By means of what is often termed "self-fulfilling prophecy," we can actually help a person become a "slow learner," a "klutz," or a "winner." Although it may be claimed that this is a "harmless" use of metaphorical language, the far-reaching effects of such activity entirely obviate such a claim. Words have consequences.

> The most important claim we have made so far is that metaphor is not just a matter of language, that is, of mere words. We shall argue that, on the contrary, human *thought processes* are largely metaphorical. This is what we mean when we say that the human conceptual system is metaphorically structured and defined. Metaphors as linguistic expression are possible precisely because there are metaphors in a person's conceptual system.[10]

In a deeper and broader sense, we can see the Orphic character of language operative at the theoretical level of human experience. Within the various language-games that form our distinctively human form of life, certain conceptual frameworks exist by means of which we carry on our various sociolinguistic tasks—frameworks that shape the content as well as the form of our encounter with different aspects of reality. In the nat-

---

[10]George Lakoff and Mark Johnson, *Metaphors We Live By* (Chicago: University of Chicago Press, 1980) 6.

ural sciences, for instance, the contributions of Galileo, Newton, Einstein, Darwin, and Nils Bohr are each focused by means of a particular paradigm that serves as the axis around which physical reality is understood. The same can be said for the contributions of thinkers in other fields, such as social science (Marx, Freud, Skinner), the arts (Plato, Nietzsche, Croce, Duchamp), and epistemology (Descartes, Hume, Kant, Bergson).

At a still more comprehensive level, this same Orphic quality of language functions with respect to what might be called the "root metaphors" funding given forms of human existence across historical and cultural boundaries. For example, the differences between the worlds of primal peoples and ancient cultures, on the one hand, and medieval and technological civilization, on the other, can be attributed to distinctive visions of the world and how human beings fit into it. In the same way, the contrast between Eastern and Western modes of thought and life largely stems from different orientations toward what it means to exist authentically in the cosmos.

To be more specific, if one conceives of one's relationship to the earth as that of a partner, rather than a foreman, then the world itself will be experienced quite differently. In like manner, if history is construed as following a cyclical pattern, as opposed to a linear progression, then our temporal life and all that is connected to it will be encountered accordingly. More crucial for our theme, if reality is approached as something that exists independently of the knower and the knowing process, then our understanding of it will take a dualistic form. Finally, if life itself is conceived of as a battle, as distinguished from a game, a party, or a journey, this will largely determine how we go about living it.

The general point here is that the relationship between language and reality is not one of mere representation and designation. The language we acquire and adopt, with various root metaphors and conceptual orientations inherent within it, directs and colors the way we construe and interact with the world around us. Although the motto "seeing is believing" characterizes the relationship between our experience and our beliefs, at a more fundamental level the motto "believing is seeing" is a more accurate characterization of this relationship.

The crucial thought to bear in mind is that we acquire our world when and as we acquire our native language. Thus, the nature of the process of acquiring a language is fundamental to an understanding of the relation between words and reality. The remainder of this section will be devoted to an examination of the dynamics of this process, by way of establishing the creative or constitutive character of speech in relation to what we know as the world. I shall conclude this examination with some remarks concerning how these reflections bear on the question of transcendence.

The main themes of Wittgenstein's later work are common knowledge. He invited us to look at language, not as a one-dimensional representation of states of affairs, but as a multidimensional, open-ended medium for accomplishing specific tasks in concrete contexts. He has suggested that the primary unit of signification is not the individual, isolated utterance but the broader context of social activity within which an utterance is used—what he termed the "language-game." These language-games overlap and criss-cross each other in exceedingly complex and fascinating ways, giving rise to linguistic modification and innovation on the one hand, and provoking and bewitching those who study language on the other hand. These language-games find their common ground and justification in the human "form-of-life," the behavior patterns that characterize our shared way of being-in-the-world. Language and action are inextricably woven together to form the fabric that constitutes both our prehension of and knowledge of the world.

These are familiar enough notions with respect to the *nature* of language, but rarely are they explored in relation to the *acquisition* of language. The base camp for such explorations must be the fundamental Wittgensteinian insight that language is, after all, an activity-centered phenomenon. It is not composed of isolated statements standing alone or joined together in static inferential sequences of a deductive or inductive nature. Rather, language arises in social contexts where speakers, as persons engaged in intentional and complex activity, seek to accomplish certain tasks. In this sense, language can be thought of as a *tool* and meaning can be seen as a function of *use*.

One important ramification of this radical shift in our understanding of language is the seemingly obvious fact that children acquire their mother tongue in the everyday push and pull of task-oriented human life. They are not given certain words to learn, along with specific definitions (whether lexical or ostensive). No, from the very first day—or before!—they are spoken to as if they are already members of the linguistic community. In spite of the fact that they do not understand a single word or sound, tiny infants are addressed, questioned, and responded to as if they do understand. And it is only because they are spoken to in this way that they come to participate in language at all.

Long before they are taught the meanings of specific terms and expressions, small children are exposed to the linguistic activity of others and participate in the speech dimension of the give-and-take, task orientation of daily life. Not only are they given simple commands and answers ("stop," "no"), but they are asked questions ("How are you today?," "What do you want?"), given requests ("Please don't do that," "Would you come over here?"), and explanations ("Do it like this," "This is hot"). In all of these cases, the meaning of the utterances is completely beyond the child. Nevertheless, their *functional meaning* is soon grasped by means of the pragmatic interaction between the speakers, the physical/social setting, and their own responses. One can learn, indeed *must* learn, the meaning of such expressions as "Don't walk on the rug" and "Bring me the book" long before learning the definitions of the terms constituting them. It is only by means of the former that the latter can be learned, for apart from a perceptual and behavioral context, it is impossible to grasp definitional meanings.

It is often argued that the bedrock from which language builds is *ostensive definition*. That is, by means of pointing to, touching, or moving various aspects of reality a speaker is able to convey the meanings of the words representing these aspects. However, Wittgenstein makes it clear that: (1) we do not learn the meanings of individual words prior to learning the meanings of entire sentences and, more important, the meanings of the language-games in which they are employed; (2) the act of pointing itself is part of a complex linguistic activity that cannot be learned by means of pointing; and (3) the meanings of such common terms as *here* and *there*, *this* and *that*, and *now* and *then* can only be learned in situ because they are relative to the speaker's location in space and time and cannot be pointed at.

The mention of space and time allows a transition to the main ideas of Maurice Merleau-Ponty as they bear on the question of language acquisition.[11] The fulcrum of Merleau-Ponty's phenomenological treatment of the human way of being-in-the-world is the notion of embodiment. After offering a systematic critique of both empiricist and rationalist accounts of perception and understanding, Merleau-Ponty posits the body as the axis of all human experience and knowledge. He contends that it is only in and through our bodily mobility and interaction with other physical objects and human bodies that we both structure our world and come to know it. The world is not observed passively as a static framework, but

---

[11]*Phenomenology of Perception* (New York: Humanities Press, 1962).

is rather encountered by means of our reaching out for and participating in it.

Each individual's induction into language follows a similar pattern. Merleau-Ponty agrees with Wittgenstein that language must be understood as a mode of behavior, not in the Skinnerian sense, but in the pragmatist sense of getting jobs done in social reality. Just as our bodies serve as the axis of our interaction with the physical world, so our speech functions as the pivot point of our existence vis-à-vis other persons. Moreover, Merleau-Ponty even stresses the Wittgensteinian theme that our language does not represent thought, but rather expresses or "accomplishes" it. Language is viewed as an extension of our embodied existence, for not only is it impossible without a body (speech-producing and hearing organs), but it frequently serves as a way of altering the environment (getting the door closed, making agreements, evoking feelings).

Meaning, according to Merleau-Ponty, is *mediated* in and through our speech-acts and their accompanying embodied behavior. It is not deduced or constructed from linguistic symbols as from some pre-established code systems. Children do not first establish that adults are speaking a language and then set about discovering how it works, as we generally do when we learn a second language. Meaning is neither read *off* nor read *into* language, but is rather *encountered in* it. Both of these last two stressed words are important. Meaning is "encountered" in the sense that we are engaged by it rather than merely exposed to it. And we encounter it "in" language because while it is more than vocabulary and syntax (is "transcendent" to them), it cannot be grasped apart from them (is "immanent" in them).

Merleau-Ponty affirms that we come into the world as "meaning-seeking" beings. In our bodies we reach out for significance; we do not wait for it to confront us. We wriggle, twist, grasp, and kick by way of interacting with and discovering our physical environment. Tiny infants have been shown to distinguish real human faces from pretend ones (and their mothers' faces from those of other persons, as well!) and to be able to mimic their mothers' sticking out their tongues.[12] In like manner, we come into the world seeking symbolic significance. We make sounds, listen for them, imitate them, experiment with them, and even invent them from the very outset. Speech, as an extension or mode of our bodily form

---

[12]Andrew Maltzoff and M. K. Moore, "Imitation of Facial and Manual Gestures by Human Neonates," *Science* 198 (October 1977): 75-78.

of life, is our way of moving around in "social space," which is—along with physical space—a complementary dimension of the world rather than a separate domain.

For Merleau-Ponty, speech, as well as bodily activity, is to be understood in terms of the notion of intentionality. Our consciousness is not only always consciousness *of* something, but our reality is both constituted and experienced as meaningful. Thus we both act and speak in the world as intentional beings, as persons who expect, find, and create meaning and significance through interaction with other embodied persons in spatial and historical contexts. It is this fabric of intentionality into which children are born, and they acquire language by being woven into it by those who are already part of it. Neither mere exposure nor intellectual capacity can account for this phenomenon. Embodied social interaction—as anticipated, expressed, and participated in—forms the matrix from within which language arises.

There are two specific aspects of language that Merleau-Ponty singles out as especially crucial to this acquisition process. The first is *onomatopoeia* and the second is *gestural meaning*. There is an actual physical connection between language and the world in the former instance, all the way from imitating nonhuman sounds in the environment to the tone and "feel" of such words as *hit, kick, smooth,* and *babble* and their counterparts in other natural languages. In the latter instance, facial expressions, bodily gestures, and tone of voice are not arbitrarily associated with certain utterances, but generally form an integral part of the meaningful gestalt of context. Children interact with these so-called nonlinguistic features of the communication process as much as with the symbol system. Apart from an encounter with these features, a child would not be able to acquire language.

Finally, let me return to the work of Michael Polanyi for a cognitive schema that both coordinates many of the forgoing emphases and provides some fundamental insights of its own. As we saw earlier, there are two major thrusts in Polanyi's epistemological investigations: the one concerns the *legitimacy* of tacit knowing and the other its *primacy*.

Polanyi proposes that we view the cognitive dimension of human experience as composed of a continuum between two poles, that of explicit knowing and that of tacit knowing. The former arises out of the interaction between focal awareness and conceptual activity. When our attention is focused on discrete aspects of our sociophysical environment and we construe them in terms of intellectual categories (as data, concepts, inferences, theories, and the like), then we can be said to be engaged in explicit knowing. Herein we seek to be as analytic, precise, logical, and objective as possible, and we recognize as knowledge only that which can be articulated and defended. These concerns have become the hallmark of cognitive responsibility in the West and have proven their value by enabling us to ferret out superstition, authoritarianism, and all manner of conceptual confusions.

Tacit knowing arises out of the interaction between what Polanyi calls "subsidiary awareness" and bodily activity. All focal awareness is grounded in and only makes sense against the backdrop of subsidiary awareness. For example, the reader is focally aware of the meaning of the sentences I have written, while being only subsidiarily aware of the specific terms and grammatical structures being used. In other words, our awareness has a "from-to" or vectorial structure: in order to attend to things in a focal sense, we must be able to attend *from* other things in a subsidiary sense. When we make physical judgments about various aspects of our world (whether about the location of the coffee table when walking through a dark living room, or the trajectory of a fly ball we are supposed to catch, or the meaning of an unfamiliar sound in the next room), we participate in and exhibit what Polanyi calls tacit knowing.

This tacit dimension of our cognitive experience is not characterized in the same way as the explicit dimension. Rather, it is rooted in what Polanyi calls "indwelling," bodily interaction with the subsidiary features of our surroundings, by means of which they become extensions of our own agency in the world. The meaning-gestalts that are formed by means of our indwelling certain features of our own environment are the result of an *integrative act*. The logic of an integrative act, unlike that of an inferential process, is irreversible in the sense that once closure is reached, the prehender cannot return to the epistemic doubt that existed before closure was reached. It's the difference between retracing the steps of a syllogistic argument and trying *not* to see a puzzle-picture once you have "seen" it.

A simple example of tacit knowing in which indwelling and integrative acts are clearly present is that of learning to drive a stick-shift automobile. One attends *from* the coordination level already achieved in one's body (an exceedingly complex level, it should be noted) *to* specific tasks of manipulating features of the immediate environment (initially experienced as isolated realities), by way of incorporating them into an integrated, meaningful whole. At each successive stage of integration, what were isolated tasks receiving our focal attention become woven into a larger whole. It is this whole *from* which we attend as we attend *to* the next task to be incorporated into the whole. Clutch, accelerator, gear-shift, and steering wheel all must be integrated into a single activity that we call "driving the car." The key to this process of integration is not that of explicit knowing, of precise definition and conceptual formulation, but is rather a function of participation, of indwelling. There is no substitute, as with swimming and other activities, for simply engaging in the activity of driving itself, "pretending" that we are driving until we find that we are. And once we know how to drive, we cannot reverse the process and begin again as if we did not know how to do it.

Coming to know another person, finding one's way around in a large city or forest, and feeling one's way into a new field of study are all exam-ples of tacit knowing at a much more complex level. In each case we bring who we are and what we already know into a diffused field of unknown particulars. Through our participatory interaction (indwelling) with these particulars at a subsidiary level of awareness, they are incorporated into our meaning-constellations through integrative acts and thus become part of the fulcrum for our continued explorations and acquisitions.

This brings us to the second main thrust of Polanyi's work, namely the more radical notion that tacit knowledge is not only legitimate but is in fact primordial. Polanyi argues that all explicit knowing is and must be grounded in tacit knowing, since the former is dependent, both logically and experientially, on a context and a vectorial perspective that can only be supplied by a prior and conceptually different epistemological footing. It is only by relying on unarticulated factors that we can articulate others, whether we are dealing with meanings or reasonings. Moreover, at the deepest level our common commitment (what Polanyi calls "universal in-tent") to the activity of acquiring knowledge about ourselves and the world, and to communicating that knowledge, can itself neither be fully articulated nor substantiated. At the primordial level our cognitive and valuational activities are symbiotic, and all of our endeavors at the ex-plicit conceptual level are dependent thereon.

Now, to return to the question of language acquisition. From a Polan-yian perspective, it seems clear that children, beginning as newborn in-fants, are immersed in the medium of language. They come to indwell social reality through their "enlargement" in much the same way that they come to indwell physical reality through embodiment. At first this im-mersion is strictly at a subsidiary level, although it is a mistake to think of it as a passive kind of exposure. The world "comes at" a child, both physically and verbally, and the child comes into the world seeking meaning and making judgments. As the child interacts physically, speech at first is strictly a force of physical behavior, with a diffuse, undifferentiated sea of sounds and accompanying activity. Later certain integrative acts occur that in turn provide an axis around which further meaning-closures begin to form. From this tacit base a child moves toward explicit articulation in speech, at first in terms of requests, responses, names, and questions, then in terms of declarations, inventions, puns, and conversation, and later in terms of concepts, rules, and reasonings.

The crucial factor in a Polanyian treatment of language acquisition is the notion of tacit knowing as rooted in subsidiary awareness and bodily activity and as providing the fulcrum for all explicit knowing. The empiricist or behaviorist account emphasizes mere exposure and physical response, failing to incorporate either the subsidiary character of the child's linguistic awareness or the embodied intentionality of the speaking community. The rationalist or structuralist account stresses the equipment or capacities with which the child encounters linguistic reality, but neglects both the crucial role of bodily activity as the matrix of linguistic meaning and the task-centered orientation of the speaking community. Thus Polanyi's schema provides a way of incorporating the strengths while avoiding the weaknesses of these two main yet conflicting schools of thought.

Polanyi has constructed an epistemological perspective that grounds cognition itself in our embodied existence, thereby shedding a great deal of light on the role of embodiment in language acquisition. How we got from ground zero, as nonlinguistic beings, to square one of the linguistic community is to be found in those tacit, integrative acts that result *from* our bodily (both verbal and nonverbal) interaction with intentional, task-centered activity (both verbal and nonverbal) of our social community and that result *in* our ability to focus specific linguistic patterns and tasks, thereby participating in that same community.

To stress exposure and reinforcement à la Skinner is not sufficient, nor is stressing the structure of the human mind, à la Chomsky. What is needed is an emphasis on the dynamic interaction between such factors at the intersection of *intentional embodiment* (following Merleau-Ponty) on the one hand and task-centered, *social interaction* (following Wittgenstein) on the other. The child comes into the world with certain capacities *and* expectations (intending meaning), and the world surrounds the child with certain patterns *and* expectations (tasks and commitments). The two indwell each other through their mutual embodiment, both linguistic and nonlinguistic, and the child forms and builds on certain integrative acts that provide both its entry point into and its leverage point within the linguistic dimension of existence.

In conclusion, we can see that our language is acquired by means of our participation in the world, and our world is acquired by means of our participation in language. Moreover, and this is my main point, both our language and our world are acquired by means of a mediational process, in and through each other by way of our interactive participation. Even as the various dimensions of reality are all transcendent to a newborn infant, but become accessible through the mediation of speech and embodiment, so too the spiritual dimension of experience can be understood as mediationally transcendent, as *beyond but within* the other dimensions.

The relationship between language and reality, between words and the world, is mediational in character and thus provides both exemplification and substantiation of the concept of transcendence. What is needed for the recovery of the notion of transcendence is an understanding of it that avoids both dualism and reductionism, even as the pattern and principles of language acquisition, and thus "world-acquisition," avoid the dualism of Chomskian rationalism and Skinnerian behaviorism.

4. Words and Metaphors

The aspect of language that primarily communicates mediated dimensions of experience is the "metaphoric mode." Analogy, paradox, irony, and the like, including of course metaphor itself, together form a category of linguistic use especially designed for speaking about these dimensions that transcend the more common and less mediated ones. As a dimension of experienced reality increases in richness and comprehensiveness, from the physical dimension to the aesthetic and moral, for instance, our efforts to communicate about it become increasingly dependent on metaphor.

What I offer here are some musings on the character of metaphor. The general background is supplied by a great deal of reading and thinking about what others have had to say about metaphor, together with a certain amount of writing on the subject. Most of the following notes mark phenomena and insights that have not been taken up in the standard literature. They are offered, not as any sort of final word, but as a helpful word along the way.

When I was in Greece, I was amused by the fact that the little three-wheeled delivery trucks that are used to transport various merchandise around the narrow city streets have a sign above the cab that reads, quite literally, in Greek: "Metaphor." The more I thought about this image in relation to the nature of metaphorical speech, the more I came to prefer it over those presented by such helpful and thoughtful thinkers as Philip Wheelwright, I. A. Richards, and Max Black.[13] To be sure, each of these thinkers had some insight into the "transfer" notion when they spoke of "diaphor," the "vehicle," and "interaction." Nevertheless, it seems a lot more mileage can be got out of this image, with respect to how metaphors function, than can be got from these by-now-standard approaches.

One way to go with this transfer image is to think in terms of the vehicle and the cargo. Here the metaphorical expression could be said to transport the meaning from one place to another. The obvious difficulty with this is that the vehicle and its cargo are separable in a way that the meaning and the metaphoric expression are not. Another way is to suggest that it is the hearer that gets transferred from one place—or one meaning—to another. But, of course, the little trucks do not transport people, only things. And yet it is people who send the things to other people, much as it is speakers who get things done by speaking metaphorically to other persons. The metaphor can be said to be the bearer of the speaker's meaning to the hearer as the truck is the bearer of cargo from one merchant to another.

In order to follow up on this theme, I examined the use of the term *metaphor* in an analytic Greek lexicon.[14] "Meta" is, of course, a most protean preposition, its meaning ranging from "with" in the genitive case to various accusative-case variations on "after." In most of the compound verbs in which it appears, it signifies some dimension of change, being linked with verbs that involve alteration—thus *metabola* (to throw), *metagrapho* (to transcribe), *metago* (to guide), *metabaino* (to move), *metamorpho* (to transform), and *metaneo* (to change one's mind or repent). "Metaphor" itself comes from the verb "phero," which means to carry. In all of these instances, the preposition would seem to indicate agency or mediation along with, or by means of, the activity in question.

Thus the use of the term *metaphor* as the name or description of the delivery truck seems all the more appropriate. The more common use of

---

[13]Cf. P. Wheelwright, *Metaphor and Reality* (Bloomington: Indiana University Press, 1962); I. A. Richards, *The Philosophy of Rhetoric* (Oxford: Oxford University Press, 1936); Max Black, *Models and Metaphors* (Ithaca: Cornell University Press, 1962).

[14]William F. Arndt and F. Wilbur Gingrich, *A Greek-English Lexicon of the New Testament* (Chicago: University of Chicago Press, 1957).

a linguistic expression is being altered in order to transform the meaning from one semantic "domain" to another or, rather, to transport the hearer from one "logical place" to another. The basic idea would seem to be that of transfer, some actual traversing of conceptual space. The metaphoric expression carries us from where we are to a fresh avenue of possibility.

This notion of the transfer of meaning is an extremely fruitful one. I have been struck by how important it is in a child's acquisition and development of speech. After having been told that the dog is a "bow-wow," the neighbor's child proceeds to identify every medium-sized, four-legged creature as a "bow-wow." When confronted with a new aspect of reality, she makes use of the linguistic tools she has to deal with it, incorporating new things into her world by transferring or extending meaning from one feature to another. This is a natural and absolutely essential step in our meaningful interaction with the world.

In this connection let me relay an experience I had with my own son when he was sixteen months old. He was sitting on my lap holding a basketball. He leaned down to bite the basketball, looked up at me and laughingly said, "Apple." Because he was well aware of the difference between apples and basketballs—he had been to many games, watched games on TV (even providing commentary: "bounce," "pass," "shoot"), and had his own hoop—it was perfectly obvious that he was not engaging in simple transfer of meaning. Rather, he was making a joke—and inventing a metaphor at the same time! The common assumption that metaphorical speech is an optional or ancillary feature of linguistic communication simply will not hold up.

There are people doing research on the use of metaphor among children. One aspect of Project Zero in Boston has been the exploration of metaphoric speech in relation to preschool children as compared with primary and secondary school students, respectively. Their findings indicate that prior to entering school, children wheel and deal with metaphor very comfortably; they enjoy puns, stories, and riddles, as well as engaging in pretending, fantasizing, and simple word games.[15] They are not threatened by verbal play and make up words of their own. Once in school, however, any sort of deviation from "standard" linguistic activity becomes increasingly threatening to children. Thus it is that during high school students have to be reintroduced to metaphorical language, a process that is both painful and only partially successful.

---

[15]Cf. *On Metaphor*, ed. Sheldon Sacks (Chicago: University of Chicago Press, 1978).

Another, related study concerns the way bilingual children compre-
hend stories told to them in languages from fundamentally different language families.[16] When the stories were told to these children in English,
which is a noun-centered (substance-attribute) Indo-European language,
the left hemispheres produced peaceful alpha waves. Alternatively, when
the same stories were told in Navajo, which is a verb-centered, more metaphoric language, the right hemispheres of their brains were active and
the left ones gave off alpha waves. Split-brain research correlates left-
hemisphere activity with analytic, sequential, and factual reasoning and
right-hemisphere activity with integrative, associative, and spatial reasoning. In this light, it would seem that metaphoric thought and speech
are no less fundamental than the so-called literal mode. In fact, to the degree that the more integrative, *gestalten*-oriented functions are primordial, to the same degree the metamorphic mode must be foundational as
well.

There is a linguistic phenomenon in the black community that provides an additional line of approach to our understanding of metaphor.
It is known as "signifying," in which one or more speakers will carry on
a conversation about a given topic by means of a conversation about a quite
different topic, all without an explicit signal or instructions. By means of
the context, a whole discourse is used to speak metaphorically about a
subject that may or may not have been established, quite apart from any
conventional lines of connection with the ostensible subject matter. Frequently this technique is used to speak about matters sexual (and, unfortunately, in a dehumanizing manner), but it is not confined to such
topics, either in theory or in practice.

Once, while standing on a street corner in Memphis, I witnessed a
typical example of "signifying." A group of young black men were standing around talking about the difficult job situation, when several young
black women walked past. Immediately, with no comment whatsoever,
the topic of conversation switched to horses and their various features and
capacities. None of the remarks was directed at the young women, nor
at any time was a correlation drawn between horses and women. The
context itself controlled this metaphorical conversation, for when the
women had passed out of sight the men returned to talking about un-
employment just as abruptly as they had stopped talking about it. By

---

[16]Linda Rogers et al., "Hemisphere Specialization and Language," *Conference on Human
Brain Function*, ed. D. O. Walter (Los Angeles: UCLA Brain Institute, 1976).

means of this contextual juxtapositioning, they had signified those women, albeit metaphorically, by speaking about horses.

In the sixties there was a popular song by a black singer named Wilson Pickett called "Mustang Sally." In fact, recent television ads for the Ford Mustang trade on the memory of this song by concluding with the question, "Isn't that right, Sally?" Anyway, the theme of this song is found in the following lines: "I bought you a brand new Mustang, a 1965. Now you come around and signify, honey, that you aren't gonna let me ride." The way she drives the car and refuses to allow the singer to enjoy it signifies the fact that he is no longer allowed the sexual privileges with Sally that he once had. The "easy rider," an expression used to refer to a pimp who need not pay for sexual privileges, no longer finds the riding so easy.

Perhaps the most interesting thing about the song is the lack of explicit connection between the two subject matters. The copula—the "is" through which similarity is affirmed—is entirely absent. Nearly all of the standard and by now well-known accounts of metaphor, from Max Black through Paul Ricoeur to John Searle, in one way or another maintain that this affirmation is essential to metaphorical utterances. However, in "signifying" the connection is implicit, being grasped in and through the context and use. There are other cases of metaphor in which the lack of a copula is even more pronounced. I shall return to this issue a bit later.

One aspect of the above considerations can be treated at this juncture by mentioning John Searle's analysis of metaphor.[17] Early on in contemporary discussions of the nature of metaphor, it became important to acknowledge that it is not very helpful to speak of *words* as metaphorical; rather, we must speak of whole *statements*. Metaphorical expressions were considered assertions in themselves, involving cognitive potential and not just rhetorical adornment. Similarly, following Searle, it has now become necessary to acknowledge metaphorical utterances as "speech-acts" in which the *use* of the statement or expression constitutes its meaning. The proposition itself (for example, "Los Angeles is a zoo") is locutionarily inappropriate, but the use to which it is put (its illocution) makes it meaningful metaphorically.

This way of putting it, of course, goes back to J. L. Austin's notion of speech-acts. It is surprising that no one has worked up a full-scale treatment of metaphorical usage employing Austin's threefold analysis of

---

[17]Cf. John Searle, "Metaphor," in *Expression and Meaning* (Cambridge: at the University Press, 1979).

speech-acts in terms of locutionary, illocutionary, and perlocutionary forces. The former (standard meaning) is clearly and deliberately crossed up by the illocutionary thrust being put in a metaphorical mode; in a way, it might be said that two locutions are fused together by the illocution. A great deal also depends upon the perlocutionary force (response) of the hearer(s). This deliberate short-circuiting of the locution in a metaphorical illocution is meant to be grasped as just that by the one(s) whom the speaker is addressing.

Now we have followed the family tree all the way back to Wittgenstein, with his emphasis on the pragmatic and social character of language. Clearly, the meaning of a metaphorical expression must be found in its context, for no grammatical or definitional analysis of the statement itself will ever reveal it. Perhaps the apex of this type of expression is the ironic utterance, since in it the locutionary force is not only crossed up, it is intentionally reversed. In irony one *says* the very opposite of what one *means*. Irony is the epitome of metaphor.

While speaking of Wittgenstein, allow me to make a few more observations apropos his understanding of language as it bears upon the meaning of metaphor. One of his insights concerned the way in which the different uses of a term or an expression are related, not by sharing a common, essential meaning, but by a series of criss-crossing and overlapping similarities that Wittgenstein called "family resemblances."[18] As the members of a family may look like each other without all sharing a common characteristic, so the different uses of a term can be related without having a common meaning. Aside from being a highly illuminating metaphor in and of itself, this notion of family resemblance can cast a great deal of light on how metaphorical speech actually works.

We may think of metaphorical speech as a means of giving expression to various family resemblances discovered in the give-and-take of human experience. Indeed, metaphor is frequently a means of establishing such resemblances by helping us see familiar features in a quite different way, a way that invites us to use our imagination. In fact, this very metaphor itself, along with a whole host of Wittgensteinian expressions, is an excellent case in point.[19] Not only would we not have thought to see connections in the ways language works and the ways members of a family

---

[18]*Philosophical Investigations*, #65-71.

[19]Cf. Jerry Gill, *Wittgenstein and Metaphor* (Washington: University Press of America, 1981).

look alike, but we have to stretch our categories in order to make it work. Unfortunately, often we suffer from hardening of the categories and resist such innovations.

I once collected expressions that employ the term *hand* in order to illustrate this notion of family resemblance in linguistic meaning. The list included such terms as *secondhand, underhanded, hand in hand, hand-to-mouth, handy, handsome, offhand, hands down,* and *hand over fist,* with many variations on each theme. The point is that these terms, and the many metaphorical uses to which they are put, do not share in a common, definitive meaning (since many of them actually have nothing to do with physical hands). Rather, each arises as a fresh way to employ a term or expression. The connection is not an extension of the former meaning, but rather an organic reproduction that takes on a life of its own.

Another Wittgensteinian metaphor that will help us find our way about here is that of the ancient city. In *Investigations* Wittgenstein speaks of ordinary language as being like an ancient city at the center of a metropolis.[20] The streets run in odd yet practical patterns, the architecture is diverse, and various features seem quaint and cumbersome. Nevertheless, it is here that people initially lived and worked, even while they built the surrounding suburbs, with their well-planned facilities and evenly laid out streets. In Wittgenstein's view, it is the diversity and complexity of the "old city" at the center of ordinary speech that functions as the ground of meaning. All trips to the clarity and order of the "suburbs" (the sciences, et cetera) must begin and return here. In Wittgenstein's early work, the *Tractatus,* meaning was defined in terms of a precisely planned mission compound separated from the wild jungle of meaninglessness by an impassable fence.[21]

The difficulty here, with respect to metaphor, is that the thinkers who work in the suburbs come to think of it as their natural home, or at least as the ideal dwelling place. Thus they think they can do without the old city, at worst calling for urban renewal (à la Russell and Carnap) and at best regarding it as a quaint "recreational" area. When such folk turn their attention to metaphor, they maintain either (1) that metaphorical speech is simply an "emotive excursion" into the wilds that lie beyond the objective suburbs or (2) that it is an attempt to lay the rough but nec-

---

[20]*Philosophical Investigations,* #18.

[21]*Tractatus Logico-Philosophicus* (London: Routledge and Kegan Paul, 1961).

essary groundwork for future suburban expansion. Thus the things affirmed by means of metaphor are said to be built upon the meanings established by literal (suburban) speech and are reducible to them without cognitive loss.

This approach to metaphor is erroneous for two reasons: (1) it fails to acknowledge that the suburbs themselves are parasitic on the old city (thus it mistakenly maintains that precise speech is logically prior to imprecise speech); and (2) it fails to see that not all excursions to the yet uncharted lands beyond the suburbs are direct extensions of literal language (thus it overlooks the important role of metaphors and models in pioneering scientific exploration). This latter point has been well handled by the likes of Max Black, Paul Feyerabend, and Thomas Kuhn, so I shall not pursue it here.[22]

Precision cannot be logically prior to imprecise speech for the simple reason that an infant would never be able to acquire language—indeed, language would never have been able to get started in the first place. The first move in speech, whether in the individual or in the species case, must be one that involves both ambiguity and vagueness. Thus the ambiguity built into metaphoric speech is not *added on* to literal utterances, but is rather part and parcel of the very matrix out of which language is born.

In modern philosophy we have been, as Wittgenstein says, "held captive by a particular picture" of linguistic activity, one implying that absolute precision is both possible and necessary to the communication of meaning. At the very least, we assume that greater precision is always desirable. In fact, absolute precision is neither possible, necessary, nor ideal with respect to human discourse. The notion of absolute precision makes no real sense at all. Rather, what is necessary for communication is a degree of precision sufficient for accomplishing the task at hand, whatever it may be. *Sufficient* precision is the proper criterion for meaning, as our earlier discussion of Alan Pasch made clear.

This calls to mind the "open-textured" character of language, and this characteristic is very much at the heart of metaphorical speech. Not only is every utterance capable of wider and more narrow specification and modification, but language itself is constantly changing and growing. New words and modes of expression are continually being introduced, while

---

[22]Cf. Black, *Models and Metaphors*, esp. chs. 1, 3, and 13; Thomas Kuhn, *The Structure of Scientific Revolutions* (Chicago: University of Chicago Press, 1970); and N. R. Hanson, *Patterns of Discovery* (Cambridge: at the University Press, 1958).

others are constantly being left behind or recycled. Metaphor exists at the cutting edge of this evolutionary process; it does not come along after and build on established meanings simply for the purposes of adornment. Rather, by means of metaphorical insight and expression, we expand the range and the depth of our understanding of the world.

A somewhat different way to put all this is suggested by Owen Barfield.[23] He maintains that most people who theorize about metaphor affirm two mutually exclusive positions. On the one hand, they contend that metaphorical utterances are parasitic on literal speech, providing a kind of creative embellishment and diversity. On the other hand, they espouse the idea that whereas primitive peoples trafficked in mythopoetic speech, in modern times we have advanced, by means of science, to a higher level of precision and analytic accuracy. Now, both cannot be true. Either literal and exact speech must come first, with metaphor following along after, or metaphorical speech must come first, giving rise to increased precision as the need arises.

Barfield himself suggests that actually there are three kinds of metaphor. One kind builds on established use and seeks to enhance or expand it figuratively, as in normal linguistic activity. Another kind operates at the poetic level, forging fresh interaction between reality and human understanding. When these "creative" metaphors become familiar, they operate as literal locutions. Third, and most important, "generative" metaphors provide what Thomas Kuhn might call the "cultural paradigm" from within which we experience and structure our world. Barfield claims that primal peoples relate to their world directly in this way. So the overall picture is a kind of sandwich, with poetic speech lying in between primordial metaphoric language on the bottom and everyday metaphorical activity on the top.

One could argue that this same pattern characterizes the way individuals grow into language as well. That is, an infant is introduced to speech by being immersed in it at the primordial metaphoric level. No locutions or terms have any specific meaning or reference at the outset. Vagueness and ambiguity abound, but reality is experienced and spoken of directly rather than symbolized. And yet, out of the push-and-pull and give-and-take of everyday interaction with speaking persons and nonspeaking aspects of the environment, a child moves toward increasingly specific language. This movement is rapid and thorough in a highly technical society

---

[23]Owen Barfield, *Poetic Diction* (Middletown CT: Wesleyan University Press, 1973).

like our own, but much less so in cultures that do not prize information so highly. Eventually, if a child is fortunate, he or she is reintroduced to the metaphoric mode at the poetic level. This may help redirect a child's awareness back to that primordial level of metaphor at the interface between thought and reality.

Let me return to a point mentioned earlier on, about not all metaphorical speech involving a copula. Almost invariably the examples used in philosophical discussions of metaphor are of the simplest, if not simplistic variety; and just as frequently they are brief, with little or no attention given to context, overall themes and patterns, and so forth. This is unfortunate at even the most basic level because it contributes to the general, often unspoken assumption that metaphors are occasional, sporadic phenomena, both arbitrary and optional. This interpretation is completely at odds with that presented by Owen Barfield. If Barfield is right about the deep and pervasive character of metaphoric thought and speech at the primordial level, then it is high time we began thinking about the metaphoric mode in broader and richer categories.

As a case in point, consider the remark made by an NBA coach some years ago when critics said his team was as good as eliminated from a playoff series: "The opera is not over until the fat lady sings." The connection here is supplied *by the context*, and listeners must discern it for themselves. Metaphoric speech is much more thoroughly woven into our linguistic patterns than we realize, and as long as we fail to acknowledge this fact we shall be unable to get untracked. Philosophic postures are themselves another case in point, since they too arise out of certain "root metaphors"—an interesting instance of metaphoric self-reference—to which they give expression.

At the most comprehensive level, parables, legends, and myths function as *extended* metaphors through which we generate, guide, and evaluate our ways of being-in-the-world.[24] Even the myth of objective reality and knowledge (by means of which we recognize myths for what they are) is itself based in a metaphoric understanding of visual perception. In the West, thanks mostly to Plato, to *know* is to *see*. In the final analysis, it must be admitted that even the notion of metaphor—as well as its counterpart, "literal speech"—is itself a metaphor. The one has to do with transfer and change, while the other has to do with using letters as symbols.

---

[24]For an interesting account of how this is so, see Sallie McFague, *Speaking in Parables* (Philadelphia: Fortress Press, 1975).

Finally, a brief proposal of my own. I think it can be shown that traditional accounts of metaphoric speech treat it either as (1) a magical, symbolic process that transcends rational analysis or as (2) an atomic, molecular building process based in factual discourse and susceptible to exhaustive, reductionistic interpretation. Even the so-called interactionists frequently speak as if the interaction between the generally unassociated regions of experience and language can be accounted for fully, given time and patience.

My own proposal is that we think of the metaphoric mode as one in which it is possible for intangible reality to be mediated in and through the particulars of tangible reality. The notion of mediation signifies the encountering of a comprehensive reality that cannot be known independently of those features of our experience that we can know directly. The aesthetic realities of tension and harmony, for instance, cannot be known apart from particular perceptual features—such as color, pitch, shape, tempo, and line—but neither can a full account of them be given in terms of these features. In a word, they are mediated in and through them while remaining transcendent to them.

Metaphor is helpfully understood as a mediational phenomenon in which certain intangible qualities and aspects among the various dimensions of experienced reality may be expressed by means of the context, use, and configuration of certain tangible qualities and aspects of that reality. What this means, of course, is that the meaning of a deep and rich metaphor cannot be exhausted by any amount of analysis, that there are mysteries in our experience that can only be encountered and engaged mediationally. In fact, it may well be that the nature of the metaphoric mode is itself such a mystery, one that can only be approached and appreciated indirectly. Thus there is something sad about those who keep insisting on a complete account of how and why metaphoric thought and speech work. In the words of Mick Jagger, "You can't always get what you want. But if you try real hard, sometimes you may get what you need."

This chapter has established the mediational character of language in relation to our involvement with and knowledge of persons, activity, reality, and language itself. It is through speech that our world comes alive to us and us to it; the various dimensions of the world are discerned through interaction, both behavioral and linguistic. The significance of this mediational character of speech for the notion of transcendence lies in the fact that it can serve both as an *instance* and as a *model* of a postmodern understanding of transcendence. Meaning is mediated in and through use, context, convention, and creative metaphor, thus transcending but not being separable from such factors.

Using the mediational character of speech as a model for our understanding of transcendence allows us to avoid both traditional metaphysical and epistemological dualism on the one hand and modern reductionism on the other. Specifically, to speak of a religious dimension that is encountered mediationally, known tacitly, and expressed metaphorically can now be seen as analogically appropriate when referring to the richest, most comprehensive dimension of human experience. To inversely paraphrase the early Wittgenstein, "Whereof we cannot help but speak, thereof we speak mediationally."

Six

CONCLUSION:

Divine Activity

as Mediational

After tracing out the logic of a postmodern understanding of transcendence in the previous five chapters, it is time now to bring these reflections to a close. I propose to do this by offering a brief application of the postmodern perspective to a concrete and crucial issue in contemporary theological discussion, namely that of the nature and possibility of divine action in the world. I shall use the early position of Austin Farrer as a foil by means of which to probe the issue from this fresh perspective. I am aware that in his later work, Farrer modified his position in a manner that is more in harmony with my own. The final section of the present chapter will return us full circle to the question of the recovery of transcendence.

The general purpose of Austin Farrer's deservedly well-known approach to our discernment of God's activity in the world is to ground it in our knowledge of ourselves as agents, especially as we interact with God as divine agent. In his book *The Glass of Vision*, [1] Farrer develops an account of how this overall approach applies to the concept of revelation and religious language. The "text" he chose for this book, "Now we see through a glass darkly," sounds as promising as the title. My concern is to develop a view of divine action that is in line with the theme implied by Farrer's title and text, namely one that stresses and develops the no-

---

[1](London: Dacre Press, 1948).

tion of God's revelatory action as mediated in and through various aspects of the world. In the final analysis, it is this mediational character of revelation and our knowledge of it that I find missing from Farrer's early treatment of the issues. I shall try to indicate how this is so as I make suggestions concerning how a mediational approach might be developed.

1. Divine Action as Relational

Against those who have sought to base our knowledge of God either on external "proofs" or internal "awareness," Farrer has stood foursquare in favor of a *relational* understanding.[2] He convincingly argues that just as our knowledge of our own and other selves is a function of our activity as intentional agents in the world, so our knowledge of God results from our interaction with divine agency in the context of our individual lives. Consequently, if we begin with an understanding of God as divine agent, we shall then have a firm basis for understanding the nature of God's revelatory action in the world. With all of this I am in agreement.

My difficulties begin when we take a closer look at what Farrer says about the nature of such a relational understanding of both our own and God's agency. When he specifically addresses the possibility of our knowledge of God, whether "natural" or "supernatural," he almost invariably speaks from *within* a rather narrow theological perspective. For instance, after setting up the factors and issues involved in distinguishing between the "natural knowledge" of divine agency and the "supernatural knowledge" thereof, Farrer concludes that "only by shifting our centre from ourselves to him, by communing with his mind, could we know the work of God through nature, in so far as it transcends the purposes of nature as nature."[3]

A bit further on, Farrer argues that supernatural knowledge must fit with natural knowledge, while at the same time transcending it. He concludes that "the judgment upon which faith is based is an *aestimatio* like that used in other fields. Faith leaps beyond it, but that happens too in common life; our faith in the goodwill of a friend goes beyond and leaves behind any weighing of the evidence for it."[4] Here we are given the stan-

---

[2]See esp. his *Faith and Speculation* (London: A. and C. Black, 1967) and *Finite and Infinite* (London: Dacre Press, 1945).

[3]Farrer, *Glass of Vision*, 30.

[4]Ibid., 33-34.

dard dichotomy between faith and reason without any suggestion that there might be a more constructive way to integrate them. More specifically, no attention is paid to the process whereby we discern in our friend's agency that quality of character that warrants our trust. In short, the epistemological and epistemic issues are left undeveloped.

It seems more helpful to develop the relational understanding of God's activity in the following way. The point of departure should be the relational character of all knowledge of persons, whether of ourselves, other, or God. To acknowledge this is to reject the standard epistemological dualism that has plagued philosophy almost since its inception, namely that between the knowing subject and the known object. As we have seen, this dualism begins by positing an epistemic gap between the knower and the known, leaving us with such time-worn difficulties as the existence of the external world, the self, other minds, and God. When, however, we begin with a relational view of the knowing situation, as detailed in chapter 3, the subject and the object are seen as symbiotic foci of a common reality in which no epistemic gap exists.[5]

The crucial consideration here is, of course, the *interactive* character of the relation between the knower and the known. Our personhood is embodied in our intentions and activity as we intersect and mesh with, or "cog into," those of other persons. Through this interactive process we come to know both ourselves and the selves of others.[6] To be sure, this process is not always a smooth one. We sometimes block or conflict with each other's intentions as they are embodied in our activity; sometimes the gears of human interaction grind rather than mesh.

This negative feature of our interaction with social reality—as is the case in our interaction with physical reality—allows for and explains error in our cognitive judgments. Even when things refuse to fit together according to this relational model, the subject and object are still interacting with each other; they are not separated by cognitive distance resulting from overdependence on a visual model of the knowing situation. Knowing is more a *doing* than it is a seeing in the passive sense, and this is no less true with respect to persons than it is to things.

---

[5]In this connection the work of Merleau-Ponty, esp. his *Phenomenology of Perception* (New York: Humanities Press, 1961) is particularly helpful.

[6]Cf. George Herbert Mead, *On Social Psychology* (Chicago: University of Chicago Press, 1964).

Nor is it less true with respect to the knowledge of God. Of course, Farrer would agree wholeheartedly with all, or nearly all, of this. The difficulty is that when one looks closely at the way Farrer speaks of our knowledge of God, whether through nature and reason or through revelation, there is often a mystical quality to his view of the resultant knowledge. One repeatedly gets the impression that the relational interaction between ourselves and God of which Farrer speaks all takes place in the *mind* of the knower. Our knowledge of God's will seems somehow more akin to mental telepathy than to true interaction. It is both generated and received supernaturally, albeit as mediated through various images, both natural and revealed.[7]

What troubles me here is the intellectualist and/or "internal" character of this view of our awareness of divine action. The image of knowledge by interaction is limited to the sphere of the mental or the spiritual; an *agent*, for Farrer, turns out to be relatively, if not essentially, *disembodied*. Now, this may be standard fare for traditional philosophy and theology, but it will not go very far toward overcoming the difficulties entailed in the subject/object dichotomy. What is needed is a model of divine action that actually takes the notion of mediation seriously.

2. Divine Action
as Historical and Social

My own proposal is that we view God's agency and our knowledge thereof as mediated in and through the interactive networks constituting history and community as well as through our individual intentional agency. Clearly, we come to know other persons in the give-and-take, the warp and the weft, of everyday social intercourse through time and in concrete contexts. Farrer's fundamental insight concerning the relational, agent-centered character of our knowledge of persons needs to be developed more concretely in terms of history and community before it can lead us out of the woods with respect to divine agency.

What is needed, in short, is the same sort of shift John Dewey urged when contrasting his own account of knowing with that of Kant; a real "Copernican revolution" in epistemology has not taken place until knowing is relocated from inside the individual mind to the more public arena of historical and community action. Speaking of the relation between sense and thought, Dewey puts it this way:

---

[7]Farrer, *Glass of Vision*, 28-32, 60-61.

In the Kantian scheme, the two originally exist in independence of each other, and their connection is established by operations that are covert and are performed in the hidden recesses of mind, once for all. As to their original difference, sense-material is impressed from without, while connective conceptions are supplied from within the understanding. As to connection, synthesis takes place not intentionally and by means of the controlled art of investigation, but automatically and all at once. From the experimental point of view, the art of knowing demands skill in selecting appropriate sense-data on one side and connecting principles, or conceptual theories, on the other.[8]

Surely it is in and through our involvement in social reality that we come to know each other and ourselves as agents; is not this the dimension of existence in which we would expect to encounter the activity of a divine person as well? In the Judeo-Christian tradition this point of departure has generally been assumed and frequently applied. At least since the Exodus, the concept of divine revelation has been understood in terms of the "mighty acts of God" in the history of the believing community. Correspondingly, the New Testament notion of incarnation focuses on pivotal *events* of Christ's birth, life, and death. Modern theology has been defined largely in terms of the various renderings offered of this overarching theme of God's action in the history and life of the community of believers.

An excellent example of this understanding of God's revelatory action can be seen in the drama, depicted in Acts, of how the first Jerusalem church council dealt with the question of including Gentiles in the Christian community. In and through Paul's missionary activity and Peter's vision of the "unclean animals" in juxtaposition with Cornelius's invitation, as well as the open, heated discussion of the issue at the council itself, the church leaders discerned that God was doing a "new thing"—revealing the divine will for their time and place. This same process was involved in discerning God's agency in the Exodus, the transfer of the kingdom from Saul to David, and the judgment of the early Christian community that "God was in Christ reconciling the world." Even the acknowledgment of the Scriptures as authoritative and inspired by God came as the result of this community process of mediational discernment.

On a broader epistemological scale, my point is that all knowing is both contextual and mediational. As I have argued throughout, there are those

---

[8]*The Quest for Certainty* (New York: Capricorn Books, 1960) 172.

who have made very persuasive cases for this perspective in recent years—from Peirce, James, and Dewey through Wittgenstein, and from W. V. O. Quine to Thomas Kuhn, Nelson Goodman, and Maurice Merleau-Ponty. The latter has stressed the crucial role of embodiment as the mediator of all cognitive activity, including both physical and social reality. G. H. Mead and Clifford Geertz have emphasized the pivotal significance of social interaction to the development of both persons and concepts. It is this broad interactionist and mediational perspective that enlivens the notions of revelation and divine activity from an epistemological point of view. It holds the prospect of liberating such notions from both rationalistic and scientistic imprisonment on the one hand and pietistic and ecclesiastical carte blanche on the other.

Consider these parallel instances of mediational knowing, the first from aesthetics and the second from linguistics. Our awareness of the motion or sadness in a painting or piece of music is mediated in and through the particular colors, lines, shapes of the former and the notes, beat, key of the latter. Such qualities cannot be *equated* with these particulars or with any definite set of them, yet they are clearly present "in" the artworks. We become aware of these qualities as a result of our interaction, whether visually or aurally, with the particulars of the work; nevertheless, they are more or other than the particulars. However, these qualities do not exist independently of the works, nor can they be known apart from encountering the particulars constituting them.

As was pointed out in chapter 6, our discernment of meaning in speech follows the same structural pattern. To use J. L. Austin's terminology once again, the illocutionary force of a given speech-act is conveyed in and through its locutionary and perlocutionary dimensions as they occur in specific speech situations. What one *means* is a function of *what* one says and *why*, in concrete contexts. It cannot be known apart from such factors as vocabulary, grammar, gestures, persons present, and environment, but it can in no way be reduced to a summary of such factors. Our meaning—whether informative, directive, expressive, or whatever—is mediated by means of the total linguistic context and is known by interaction with the particulars of this context, not simply by passive exposure to them.

God's involvement in the world is best construed, in my view, along the mediational and interactive lines displayed in aesthetic and linguistic discernment. To say that God acts in human existence is to call attention to certain features and contexts in which one "reads" or "encounters" a surplus of significance. The surplus is not "extra" in the quantitative sense, but is nonetheless real for being intangible. It is like momentum in an athletic contest; its effect is there even though it never appears in the box score. Those who participate in the game, whether players or spectators, sense its presence and respond accordingly.

One other point before continuing. Mediational knowledge is neither direct, as with mystical intuition, nor inferential, as logic and science is. Direct awareness is in no way dependent on intermediate processes and practices, while inferential knowledge is reversible and essentially continuous. Mediated knowledge is necessarily involved in concrete factors and circumstances without being entailed by them. Our awareness of divine agency, similarly, is mediated in and through historical and social events and dynamics, but not in a step-by-step manner. Rather, it is discerned as a result of *participatory interaction* with these events and dynamics.

3. Divine Action and Confirmation

The forgoing presentation of the general epistemological features of the mediational process brings us, finally, to the specifically epistemic issues of truth, error, and confirmation. At this point I should like to return to my second quotation of Farrer in this chapter. Therein he refers to the judgment upon which faith is based as an *aestimatio,* an estimate that arises from experience and reason but which nevertheless goes beyond them. There are at least two specific aspects of this notion that bear further discussion: the first pertains to the sense in which the rationale of such judgments must remain *unarticulated* and the second concerns the possibility of such judgments being *incorrect.*

Ever since Plato, but especially in modern and contemporary philosophy, knowledge has been equated with that which can be explicated. It has been thought of as the identification, definition, isolation, and replication of all of the elements constituting *what* is known and *why* it is claimed to be known and deemed essential. If you cannot say what you know and show how you know it, you cannot be said to "know" in the preferred sense. Generally knowledge is said to be statable in *propositional* form and supported by *inferential* (either deductive or inductive) reasoning. It is this *explicit mode* that is said to constitute the realm of "objectivity," with all epistemic claims that do not measure up being confined to the realm of "subjectivity."

Over against this dominant epistemological model stands a more heretical but more fruitful approach that begins by acknowledging, in the words of Michael Polanyi, that we always "know more than we can say." Indeed, if this were not true, we would never be able to get started saying anything about what, and on what basis, we know. The contention here is that all explicit knowing, in the propositional and inferential sense, is logically dependent upon tacit or implicit knowing grounded in our skilled and social activity. Propositions and inferential processes only arise and take on meaning within and around certain tasks, contexts, and communities that come into being prior to any articulated rationales and provide the epistemological bases for them.

The relevance of such considerations should not be difficult to grasp. If the dominant model of what constitutes knowledge is not jettisoned, there can be no hope of utilizing the notion of mediated knowledge in connection with revelation and divine agency. If, on the other hand, we adopt a model that enables us to accredit our powers of tacit discernment, then we may be in a position to show that knowledge of God's action in the world is at least meaningful and possible. If tacit knowing is accepted as logically prior to and every bit as viable as explicit knowing, then our talk of discerning God's activity in a given event or community need not be disqualified beforehand or be dismissed as dogmatic "word-salad."

Let me return to our knowledge of and language about other persons. Personal knowledge and speech clearly require and exemplify a mediational mode. The demand that all knowledge be articulatable led to what had been called the problem of "other minds," as well as to doubt about the possibility of self-knowledge. A great deal of energy has been devoted in modern and contemporary philosophy to establishing some rational connection between the knowing subject and his or her knowledge of other persons and/or the self. Everyone acknowledges that solipsism is unrealistic, but few have been able to show why.

The solution is to realize that our knowledge of other persons and our own selves is built into our very way of being-in-the-world. The embodied and linguistic character of our existence entails both a social and personal dimension of reality. We begin as beings in relationship, and by means of relationships we come to know ourselves in the world. To put it differently, the concept of "person"—whether ourselves or others—is not something we reason *to;* rather, it is that which we reason *from.* In short, as P. F. Strawson put it, the concept of a person is a "logically primitive" notion. It is mediated to us in and through our involvement with others in a common environment. Whenever we seek to articulate this knowledge in an "objective" manner, we end up begging the question, as the ironic statements of both Descartes ("*I* think, therefore I am") and Hume ("*I* am unable to find a self") clearly illustrate.

Although admittedly there are differences between thinking of God and thinking of human persons, an exploration of the common mediational character of our knowledge of each will help to resolve the question of the possibility and nature of God's action in the world. I contend that we discern God's involvement *in and through* interaction with our environment, both physical and social. Such discernment is, as Farrer says, an *aestimatio*, but this neither means that it is a blind leap of faith nor that it is an inductive inference. It is more akin to what C. S. Peirce called "abduction," John Henry Newman termed the "illative sense," and Pascal designated as "reasons of the heart."[9]

There is, of course, no guarantee that all claims to having discerned divine agency are veridical. There is always the possibility of error and/ or differences of interpretation. Nevertheless, there are also instances of widespread agreement in religious discernment, as the history and cross-cultural breadth of the world's major religious traditions clearly show. The modern, dogmatic dichotomy between the objective and the subjective does not fit the facts. Such "subjective" dimensions as art and religion, for example, frequently exhibit a great deal of consensus without denying plurality and tolerance, even as such "objective" dimensions as physics and mathematics submit more to sociopolitical dynamics and aesthetic considerations than is generally acknowledged.

The above remarks raise the question of *criteria* in relation to evaluating claims of discerning God's activity mediated in and through the historical and social dimensions of human existence. Clearly, there can be no cut-and-dried criteria with respect to any mediated knowledge. Farrer, however, speaks helpfully of three basic kinds of criteria that he calls "preparatory, intrinsic and relative." I think his list provides an excellent place to start with respect to this issue:

> The preparatory criteria are simply those of other sciences, such as history, which undertake the examination of the factual evidence. . . . the intrinsic criteria are nothing other than the character and structure of (alleged) revelatory fact, not merely as first encountered, but as added up and gone over in every part . . . as happens, perhaps, when we judge the merit of any great and original work of art. . . . The intrinsic criteria are scarcely separable from the relative—we should not find revelation intrinsically con-

---

[9]Cf. C. S. Peirce, *Values in a Universe of Chance*, ed. Philip Wiener (New York: Doubleday, 1959) 268-77; John Henry Newman, *The Grammar of Assent* (Notre Dame: University of Notre Dame Press, 1979) ch. 9; Blaise Pascal, *Pensées*, #277.

vincing if everything else made nonsense of it, and it made nonsense of everything else.[10]

To those who demand more than this, I can but (1) remind them of Aristotle's remark that we should only expect as much precision within a given area of experience as is appropriate to it, and (2) bid them reflect on the unspoken commitments that such a demand entails. The possibility of discerning God's activity in the world only makes sense, in my view, when construed in a mediational, confessional, and open-ended manner.

4. The Recovery of Transcendence

This examination of the concept of divine action in the world, offered from a postmodern point of view, is nowise to be taken as a definitive statement on the topic. It is meant, rather, as an initial sketch of how this crucial issue might be approached. Admittedly, a great deal of work remains to be done in working out the details and wrinkles.

In sum, my argument has been that the loss of transcendence resulting from atomistic analysis and epistemological dualism can be counteracted by drawing upon a model of transcendence that centers in the notion of mediation. Mediational transcendence overcomes the dualisms inherent in the modern approach to ontology, epistemology, ethics, and linguistic meaning by focusing on the participatory and interactive character of reality, knowledge, behavior, and speech.

Reality can now be understood as the intersecting of symbiotic dimensions, the richer and more comprehensive of which are mediated in and through the less rich and comprehensive. This way of construing reality avoids the traditional view of it as consisting of separate realms. Human beings exist in this matrix of dimensions as relational and interactive agents. This fresh model enables us to speak of the transcendent *within* our experience rather than beyond, above, or other than it. The traditional dichotomy between the natural and the supernatural can be set aside.

Our knowledge of the various dimensions of reality is also best construed as mediational in character. The *relational* nature of human embodied existence, arising out of interaction with our physical and social environments, yields a form of cognition necessarily grounded in *tacit*

---

[10]"Revelation," in *Faith and Logic*, ed. B. Mitchell (Boston: Beacon Press, 1957) 101-102.

knowing. Thus the justificatory processes themselves must also be a function of participation and interaction. We come to know the various dimensions of reality, as well as the loci of meaning and activity within them, by means of our involvement with them and each other. The transcendent is hence understood as knowable in the same way as, and *in and through*, the other dimensions of experienced reality.

With the loss of an absolute basis, moral values were for a time tossed about on a sea of relativity. They can now be understood as arising within the relational and contextual fabric of common human experience and intentions. They are worked out between the poles of relativity and responsibility, through dialogue and persuasion. The traditional separation between the vertical or transcendent basis and the horizontal or humanistic basis for moral values is overcome by anchoring them in our commitment to both stability and growth.

Linguistic meaning can also be rescued from the slings and arrows of outrageous dualism, by construing it as a function of relational interaction among embodied persons at work and play within common contexts and activity patterns. The traditional dualisms between word and object, sense and reference, and cognitivity and noncognitivity—each the result of a commitment to some version of the "picture-theory of meaning"—are now seen as unhelpful and misleading. Focusing on the interactive and creative quality of human speech directs our attention to the symbiotic and open-textured character of linguistic communication. Moreover, our language about those dimensions of experienced reality that are known mediationally and tacitly can now be understood as necessarily polysignificant and metaphoric. We acquire and construct our worlds in and through our participation in the speech community, and this applies to our experience of the transcendent as well.

The recovery of the transcendent, then, is both possible and actual to the degree that we acknowledge the mediational character of human existence, knowledge, and activity, while affirming our own embodied participation in these mediational processes. The transcendent is *more* than the other dimensions of existence and experience without being *other* than them. A mediational understanding of transcendence enables us to preserve the values of the traditional and modern approaches while avoiding their inherent dualisms and ensuing stalemates. At the same time, this mediational notion of transcendence allows us to profit by the insights of contemporary, postmodern thought and life while remaining open to the future.